Monica M. Johnson

Who Best to Tell My Story

An Unforgettable Journey of Hope and Healing

Amazon 2019

ISBN: 9781081206291

Table of Contents

Dedication 4

Introduction: A Story to Tell 5

1. The Black Sheep..8

2. Have Mercy on Me...16

3. How Are We to Return?...22

4. Listen to Your Father 42

5. The Raging Storm 51

6. Raised Up!...59

7. Point of No Return 73

8. The Apple of His Eye..89

9. But Now My Eyes Have Seen You 104

EPILOGUE: The Storm Is Over 118

Dedication

For Dad, Mom and my children.

"A season of suffering is a small price to pay for a clear view of God"
(Max Lucado)

Introduction: A Story to Tell

I want you to know, brothers, that the gospel I preached [tell] is not something that man made up. I did not receive it from any man, nor was I taught it; rather, I received it by revelation from Jesus Christ. (Galatians 1:11–12, NIV)

The skies were clear but a storm was brewing—a storm that would change my life forever.

It was early morning. I was driving home from working the night shift at the local hospital, Anne Arundel Medical Center, in Annapolis, Maryland. Only minutes away from my destination, Mama's house, my car slid out of control on a patch of black ice. As it skidded aimlessly from one side of the bridge to the other, I cried out in desperation: "Oh, God, please don't let me die like this! Oh, no! LORD! Please don't let me kill anyone!"

My hands became entangled as I wrestled for control of the steering wheel, but to no avail. The bumper of the approaching vehicle violently tore into the driver's side of my car.

Then silence. I heard nothing.

The car came to a complete stop.

And my life was thrown into a whirlwind.

The storm gathered force quickly.

In the shock trauma unit, the emergency medical technicians did all they could to keep me alive. With each minute that passed, my chances of survival decreased. The prognosis was death.

My injuries were numerous: a bilateral collar fracture, a shattered pelvis, a ruptured bladder and spleen, fractured ribs, a torn colon, lacerations to my kidney and liver, and a collapsed lung. My almost-lifeless body was connected to numerous machines and tubes.

Who Best to Tell My Story

People raced about around me. I could see them, but I couldn't hear a word. And I couldn't make a sound. My gaze scanned the room, trying to understand it all. Then I closed my eyes to the world. I wondered if it was time to rest forever.

But God, the Father, He was calling me to Himself with a purpose. It was not the call to eternal life. This was not the end but a beginning.

A beginning not yet fully revealed. The end of my life as I knew it.

There was a divine plan for my life, and it would alter any and all plans that I had innocently made for myself. I had never sought guidance from the One who created me. And there were gifts and talents within me that had gone unnoticed. There was greatness and strength within me that I had never tapped into. There was a person inside of me who was hidden and suppressed. I was about to embark on a journey of hope and healing—a journey that would ultimately reveal who I am and why I was created.

We learn and grow through the sharing of our life stories. Although my life story and yours are different, we're on a similar journey—a journey toward hope and healing, a journey toward God. None of us are sure where the journey will lead. But it's God's hope that the journey will ultimately help us grow closer to Him.

Along the way, our individual journeys weave in and out of others'. We all have struggles, trials, and challenges. We all sin. We all have questions about God, suffering, purpose, and destiny. Although my life story is different from yours, it's my hope that you will be able to relate to my spiritual struggles and apply the lessons I've learned to your own life. My intent is to reveal "signs" that may help you prepare for, identify, endure, and, with God's help, overcome the inevitable storms of your own life. I hope to encourage you to know and experience God as never before. To discover the power of God's Word, which can equip you to live a victorious Christian life—not free from problems but free from spiritual defeat.

Monica M. Johnson

I'm extending you an invitation to walk in my shoes for a little while. As you walk with me through this journey of hope and healing, I encourage you to consider your own journey. Together, we will discover the joys and sorrows, the pains and pleasures, the hopes and fears, and the losses and gains of simply living. There are many winding turns on this rough road, but at the end, there is God, there is victory, there is life.

1. The Black Sheep

*But you are the ones chosen by God, chosen for the high calling
of priestly work, chosen to be a holy people, God's instruments to
do His work and speak out for Him, to tell others of the night-
and-day difference He made for you—from rejected to accepted.*
(1 Peter 2:9, The Message)

Different

I'd always felt different from everyone else. In my mind, there
was no doubt that I was adopted. All my suspicions seemed to be
confirmed one day when I was twelve. I was sitting on the living
room floor of my paternal grandmother's house thumbing
through an old photo album. Something strange fell out—a birth
announcement. My birth announcement. I hesitantly read it.
There, in bold black letters that seemed raised off the page, was
my date of birth: December 22, 1968. We had always celebrated
my birthday on December 23.

I didn't look like any of my siblings. And I was constantly
reminded by others outside of the family that I was the "black
sheep," the only "dark-skinned child." My brother called me
"Blackie." I was plagued with thoughts of being different, even
ugly. I associated black with ugly. The name made me see myself
as someone rejected, disliked, and stupid.

My sisters were always told that they resembled Mama. No one
ever said that about me. Some people said I looked like my
daddy, but I couldn't see the resemblance. Whenever someone
told my sisters how much they looked like Mama, they would
smile and chuckle sweetly. I imagined it made them feel beautiful
and happy. I certainly would have felt beautiful and happy if I
were told that. But I wasn't.

Monica M. Johnson

Why couldn't people hear my cry to be adored? I just wished someone could feel my isolation and tell me something good about myself. Something to make me feel pretty—like a girl, or a princess, even. I didn't want to be told that I looked like Daddy; he was a man. Even though Mama, with her warm smile, would introduce me as the "baby girl," it wasn't enough to make me feel I shared in her beauty.

So, I grew up feeling like a tomboy. I climbed trees with the boys and protected my sister. I didn't like being a tomboy, but it just seemed like the place I fit.

This can't be true, I thought, as I looked at my birth announcement. We'd been celebrating my birthday on the twenty-third for twelve years. But the truth was right there in my hands. My heart skipped a beat and my eyes widened as I read on to find the names written at the bottom of the announcement. I held my breath for a brief moment and then exhaled with relief. *Sylvester and Brenda Johnson*. My parents. The tormenting fear was finally gone. I wasn't adopted.

After that, Mama sent away for a duplicate copy of my birth certificate to have on hand, to remind me that I wasn't adopted even though I felt different.

The relationship you have with your parents as a child is vital in shaping your destiny, whether you're the oldest, middle, or youngest. Your early perceptions of your reality have greatly influenced your current reality. My feeling of "being different" as a child played a part in shaping my journey. I heard the negative things loud and clear and became defeated in my thinking early on. I was unable to dream big, or even dream at all. I was ready to settle for whatever life had to offer me. I couldn't finish things that I started; I'd give up easily. I was willing to do without and be last because I thought others were more deserving. I expected few good things. And I anticipated only the worst. I wanted so much to be happy and feel beautiful. I wished that I could say helpful and kind words that others wanted to hear, and to be someone who made a difference in the world. Instead, I felt unimportant, unattractive, and useless.

My Family

When I recall my early childhood years, I think fondly of my father, Grafton Sylvester. Sylvester was one of nine children. His complexion was dark and smooth. He was strong and well built, with legs that bowed slightly. His stance reflected his boldness. Though he would stutter now and then, he always looked me in my eyes, wanting my full attention. His hands were big, firm, and powerful, yet he was gentle when he scolded. Daddy's discipline brought me a sense of comfort; he disciplined out of love, not anger. Daddy was great, except for one problem: he drank too much. Daddy was an alcoholic.

My mother, Brenda, was the oldest of six children. She was thin and relatively short, with a fair complexion that could almost be mistaken for Caucasian. She had beautiful black hair and sympathetic dark eyes. But it was her hands that really stood out to me. Mama's hands were soft and warm, and there seemed to be a magic in her touch. Sometimes in the middle of the night, when she was sound asleep in bed with Daddy, I would quietly push their bedroom door open, tiptoe across the floor to her side of the bed, and tap on her shoulder. She'd open one eye.

"Mommy, my stomach aches," I'd whisper. She wouldn't say a word. Instead, she'd express her thoughts through her countenance and her touch. She'd slowly lift her blanket and shift her body toward Daddy's side of the bed. This was my invitation to crawl in. Yawning, I'd rest my head on the pillow feeling reassured that Mama was going to rub the pain away. Peace would fill my heart. I don't know how she did it, but she always made me feel better. She'd place her soft, warm hands on my belly and erase the pain. Soon I'd be fast asleep, resting in the safety and comfort of my mama's arms.

Monica M. Johnson

Mama was different from her sisters and brothers as well. She was unique. Her reverence for God set her apart. She had great zeal for God. She had charisma when talking about Him, and she acknowledged Him in her daily living. Mama was always giving thanks for each new day. She gave thanks for the things we had and for the things that He would provide, to meet whatever needs arose. Her faith likely stemmed from watching her mama, Frances, and her grandma, Prudence, who also loved the Lord with all their hearts.

Mama was a giving and sensitive woman with an indescribable spirit of compassion. She was a woman who constantly gave her love, her time, her money, and anything else asked of her. She gave so much that I often questioned if she knew how to receive. She had an ability to love without conditions, and to comfort without limitations. Once when I was a child, I sat with Mama at her bedroom window watching a thunderstorm. I remember her saying, "We're watching the Lord at work." Even when it seemed like the entire house would be uprooted and destroyed, Mama focused beyond the winds and the rains. She never showed fear. She believed God was always present.

Mama married for the first time at the young age of seventeen. She and her husband had two daughters, Carmen and Nanette (Nan), and a son, Charles Junior. After several years, against all that she'd been taught by her grandmother, Mama got a divorce. Three or four years later, she met my father. It wasn't until after my sister, Vanessa, and I were born that Mama married our father.

Until I was about eight years old, we lived in the projects in Annapolis, MD, where we lived for five years. Although we lived in the city, Daddy decided that Vanessa and I would attend school in the country until our house was built. This would allow us to catch the bus from school to my granny's house until Mama was able to pick us up in the evening. Carmen, Nan, and Junior attended school in the city. They were old enough to return home until Mama or Daddy arrived. Every morning, Mama would drive Ness and me ten miles into the country to Granny's house, where we caught the bus. Then Mama had to drive another forty or fifty miles in the opposite direction to go to work. Driving to the country with Mama was always enjoyable. She used that time to talk to God (pray), and she allowed us to talk to Him along with her.

A couple of years later, we moved out of the projects to a community in the country, less than ten miles from the city, called Browns Woods. This is where our family home was built. It had four bedrooms, two baths, a family room, a living room, a dining room, a kitchen, a laundry room, and big yards in the front and back of the house. The houses here were built close together. In a backyard or two were some farm animals—pigs, chickens, cows, and even horses. There were no sidewalks. The streets were narrow and not well paved. Everyone was kin or had lived there long enough to feel like family; everyone looked out for one another. Daddy's mother also lived in this community, as well as Mama's mother and grandmother and a host of cousins, aunts, uncles, and friends. It was a good place in which to grow up.

I never referred to my siblings as half-sisters and half-brother. In fact, I never heard the term "half" until I was much older. We all called our mother "Ma" or "Mama," and much later "Bren." But my two oldest sisters and my brother never called Sylvester "Dad." He provided for all of us equally, but they didn't have the same kind of relationship with Daddy that Vanessa and I had. This wasn't a negative thing—it was just the way it was.

I don't remember spending much time with my siblings during my early years, but I remember their characteristics. A tender soul like Mama, Carmen was quiet, easygoing, and somewhat timid. Charles Jr. was carefree and happy-go-lucky. He'd go with the flow of things. Despite his rough-tough boyish disposition, he was caring and sensitive. Nan was bold, bossy, confident, and cocky. In my eyes, she was a rebel without a cause. She had her own program and wasn't the type to wait around for the family to make decisions for her. She frequently made negative comments and always had to have the last word. But once you got past her brash and sometimes seemingly bitter exterior, you would see the compassion in her heart.

I always perceived Vanessa as very beautiful, perhaps because whenever people outside of our home needed to distinguish between Vanessa and me, they would refer to her as the "cute one" or the "light-skinned one." And so I felt inferior. No matter how much attention I received, it was never enough for me. I constantly felt empty. This was the beginning of an intense need to be accepted by others and overwhelmingly low self-esteem.

Mama nurtured and loved us all. She said she had no favorites and loved us all equally. Certainly we all had different needs, and Mama met them accordingly. But if there was a favorite, in my eyes, Ness was the one. Even so, I never resented her. Always cheerful and confident, Ness was so much fun to be around. We were one year and thirteen days apart, and we did everything together. We never fought because Daddy taught us to never compete with one another. We were always encouraged to support each other. The older I grew, the more I desired to share in Ness's happy spirit and confidence. But I never felt I measured up to the great qualities that she upheld.

Malissa (Missy) and Phillip (Tucker) became my siblings at heart when Mama received them as her own. Missy and Tucker were two of five siblings. Their father and Mama's first husband, Charles, were brothers. Their mother died when Missy was still a teenager and Tucker was in his early twenties. Before their mother's death, Missy, Ness, and I played together all the time. And Junior and Tucker weren't just first cousins but also best friends. Through the years, Missy and I grew even closer. We shared secrets and fears, cried together, laughed together, and hoped together.

My other brother, Sylvester Jr., was Daddy's son. He was born before Daddy met Mama. We didn't spend much time together during my childhood. He served in the military and stayed in touch with Daddy through letters. Still, I loved him as my brother and nothing less.

Early Interactions

Throughout my childhood, I watched how Mama interacted with Daddy. I saw that she didn't share her feelings toward him with him. So I came to accept that it wasn't my place to share my feelings with others. I could feel emotions bubbling on the inside but didn't know how to put them into words. Since I was never encouraged to share my feelings, I would shut down when

I didn't understand something about the world around me. I would go to school and not ask the teacher questions. I believed that what I had to ask wasn't important to others.

Confrontation was traumatic for me. If someone confronted me, I automatically felt attacked. And again, I'd shut down emotionally instead of sharing what I was feeling. I didn't know how to express my pain. I had no model to teach me how to share my thoughts, how to dream, or how to deal with conflict. Because I didn't have a personal relationship with Mama's God (with whom she shared everything), I was at a loss.

Daily, I would scream for help as loud as I possibly could. There were times I would scream and scream until I had no breath. And I would watch my family ignore my screams and act as if everything were fine. I heard the people in church talk about God as though he was present. He didn't seem present to me. I cried inside the church and outside the church. No one heard me.

The reality was that I was only screaming within. Too afraid to cry aloud. Too intimidated to let my voice be heard. No one could hear my scream because I had no voice.

Monica M. Johnson

I felt I had no purpose. Often, I felt no need to live. I wanted the pain to end. How was I supposed to grow into adulthood when the little girl was unable to be a little girl? How was I supposed to become a beautiful woman with self-worth when defeat, ugliness, stupidity, and rejection were all I anticipated? How was I supposed to love, forgive, and respect when I didn't know the origin of these things? How was I supposed to know about purpose and destiny when survival was my theme song? How could I give others hope or wisdom if I couldn't relate to their joys and successes?

I was the black sheep. I was different.

2. Have Mercy on Me

What strength do I have, that I should still hope? What prospects,
that I should be patient? (Job 6:11, NIV)

No Stranger to Storms

The storms in my life began erupting when we lived in the
"projects." During those years, Daddy's drinking opened the door
to a pain that would later drive me into the world on a vain search
for love from others.

In my very young years, Mama and Daddy seemed good for each
other, but when I was eight years old, they began to argue for
reasons unknown to my siblings and me. At first they were
discreet. I had no clue that there was a problem. Then suddenly, it
was as if they just didn't get along anymore.

When Daddy first started drinking, he never drank in front of us.
He'd go out, get drunk, and somehow return home. Then he'd sit
on the vinyl recliner in the living room with the lights dim
listening to Motown 8-track tapes. He'd sing along, and with the
stench of liquor on his breath, he'd casually hug and kiss Vanessa
and me good night. Over the years, he gradually became
aggressive. We felt we had to tiptoe around him. When he and
Mama began arguing intensely, Mama would order us to go to
our rooms, but the intensity of their voices carried their
arguments through the walls. I would jump into my bed and pull
the covers over my head. My heart would beat rapidly but I
wouldn't cry. Fear would grip me into silence.

I always feared their arguments would escalate into a physical altercation. My worst fear was that Daddy would kill Mamma. I didn't want to imagine life without her. Daddy would get so angry that he didn't look like my daddy at times. I remember him speaking to Mama in a tone that carried a great heaviness. I never understood the purpose those harsh words served. They didn't make Mama agree with him. They never helped Daddy make his point any clearer. They only caused me to question my role in his unhappiness.

As I grew older, Daddy's drinking became a regular occurrence. My parents were no longer concerned about my siblings and me being present when they argued. I don't remember my siblings' reaction to the drinking. My memory allows me to recall only the isolation I felt. No one talked about what was happening all those years. I felt completely alone and utterly helpless. Sad and angry.

I watched Mama go to work each day as if she had no worries. But I worried about her. I listened to her when she talked to God. She spoke in a soft tone but with strong words—words that hoped for protection, longed for change, and believed in an answer.

Every Sunday before church, Mama would gather us together in the fancy living room: the one room no one was allowed to use regularly. There was no television. There was no radio. Only stiff furniture we couldn't sit on. We used this room for prayer. Sometimes Daddy would join us. Other times he was hungover and unable to get out of bed. Or maybe he felt too guilty to join us. I never knew his reasoning.

In the sacred room, we held hands as Mama looked each of us in the eyes and told us to give thanks for something that God had done for us. Mama would usually give thanks first. Then, one by one, each of us would follow suit. We would thank God for the same things: food, shelter, and clothing. Someone might thank

God for waking him or her to see another day. Our voices never sounded happy. I don't think we were actually excited about living another day in our situation—it was just something we heard Mama say a time or two. After everyone gave thanks, Mama would pray aloud with great belief that God was listening. She'd say, "A family who prays together stays together."

I stood in that prayer circle out of obedience. I didn't care if the family stayed together. I was no longer the girl who enjoyed horsey rides on Daddy's knee. Being a family was far from my mind.

After dismissing us from the prayer circle, Mama would check the food cooking on the stove and set the temperature dials on low. She would always begin preparing for Sunday dinner early in the morning—and we always had a big Sunday dinner. Then we'd leave for church. Everyone except Daddy.

I felt trapped. Trapped inside my own mind.

A Nightmare Come True

Life inside our home became increasingly difficult to deal with. There were nights I wouldn't sleep. Drunk and perhaps fueled by his inner pain and frustrations, Daddy often threatened that we would be the next family in the newspaper, burned in a house fire. I never knew why he made such a threat but he did. The nights when Daddy didn't pass out, he and Mama would fight until the "wee" hours of the morning. Some nights Daddy didn't sleep off his drunkenness, and he'd wake up and continue the same argument from the night before.

One time when he was drunk, he threw piles and piles of our clothes on the front lawn and demanded that we all get out of the house. It happened just in time for the kids on the school bus to see. Unable to hold my head up in school, I avoided eye contact with others. My nervous belly, decreased appetite, and low self-esteem made it difficult to concentrate in school. Shame, fear, and embarrassment were the ruling emotions inside of me.

Monica M. Johnson

One day, the tension at home heavy and ongoing, with my siblings all away from the house, Mama forced me to spend the day with her sister. That night, everything changed for the worse. Returning home, I saw police cars and an ambulance in our driveway. At the time, I believed that I was the one responsible for protecting Mama, so I was always afraid of leaving her alone. I was the one who was able to talk to and reason with Daddy. I was the one who would prevent him from becoming violent during their arguments. I was the one who would stand between them and stop Daddy from hurting her.

I hadn't been there this time.

Deep within my heart I'd felt the need to stay at home with Mama that day. But after several minutes of her persuading me that she'd be okay, I was given no choice but to leave. Both Mama and Aunt Bev had wanted me out of the house.

The curtains were open, revealing that the lights were on throughout the house. The front door was also open. My heart raced. Tears welled up in my eyes. I hoped my nightmare hadn't come true.

What's going on? Is Mama hurt? Did Daddy's anger get the best of him? Is Mama still alive?

My breathing was labored. My anxiety grew. I wanted to jump out of the car and run to Mama. The car seemed to be moving in slow motion. Our 150-foot driveway seemed to go on for miles. Finally, we came to a stop. I proceeded to open the door but my aunt quickly ordered me to remain in the car. Each second was an eternity. I wanted to see my mama's face and know that she was okay. My aunt cautiously moved toward the house. An officer approached her as she reached the front door. With my window rolled down, I listened as he told her what had happened. I felt my heart drop. My stomach turned, my head pounded. I felt like I was going to die.

There had been a fight. I stared at the house and into the well-lit rooms, trying to see Mama. Then, there she was, timidly walking out of the house with blood on her mouth. And part of me did die. I felt something I'd never experienced before: rage. An extreme hate for Daddy. I hated him so much that I actually wanted him dead.

As I looked into Mama's red eyes, I could almost feel her pain and fear. My heart ached. Unable to catch my breath, I began to cry uncontrollably as I got out of the car. I wanted to hold Mama close to me. I wanted her to hold me back. But she didn't. She stood close to my aunt and she seemed to have pushed me away.

And then, all I wanted was revenge. I wanted to see Daddy suffer.

As I looked around for Daddy, I heard the officer say that they were holding him in the back seat of the police car. I hadn't noticed him when we arrived. But there he sat. His eyes were bloodshot. His stare beyond the present. I stood right there in front of him. He didn't see me at all.

But I saw him. This was the second time that my daddy no longer looked like my daddy. Instead, he looked evil and ugly. And I hated the man I saw.

I don't know why, but Daddy wasn't taken away. Mama and I were escorted to my aunt's vehicle. We would stay with her until things "cooled down." After that night, I hated life even more. I hated myself all the more. I hated that I hadn't been there to protect Mama. I blamed myself for what had happened to her. I wasn't certain, but I was pretty sure Mama blamed me as well. Surely, her silence was her way of blaming me. She still hadn't embraced me.

I thought Mama would leave Daddy after that night, but she didn't. Daddy was court-ordered out of the house for fifteen days. And when he returned, things only got worse.

Monica M. Johnson

Dark Voices

We continued living in the house and didn't talk about what was happening. I didn't know how to free myself from the hate growing inside of me. I felt numb about losing either of them but hurt about feeling lost. I no longer feared the results of their fighting or someone dying because being left alone seemed to be happening while they were still present. And I was no longer Daddy's little girl. I wanted more and more to be alone, and intentionally isolated myself. In my misery, I was pretty certain that others wanted to be around me less and less as well. I no longer trusted Mama's words—"It won't be this way forever."

My thoughts were dark, and I couldn't see a reason to live. One day while at my grandmother's house, I locked myself in the bathroom and sat on the cold tile floor, my back against the door. My hands were filled with tear-saturated toilet tissue. I wanted to end the pain that rested in my chest. I wanted to silence the dark voices in my head. But I didn't know how. I sank down further. My face to the floor, I lay in the fetal position. There was a pounding on the door, and voices demanding that I come out. Vanessa urged me not to give up.

Too weak and too afraid to end it all, I began simply existing. Everyone continued on as if I were okay. I became mean. Pushed others away. Trusted no one. Believed in nothing. No one came to help. No one had mercy on me.

3. How Are We to Return?

"Ever since the time of your forefathers you have turned away from my decrees and have not kept them. Return to me, and I will return to you," says the Lord Almighty. "But you ask, 'How are we to return?'" (Malachi 3:7, NIV)

Salvation Undefined

I was a weak, miserable, insecure girl when I walked to the front of Asbury Broadneck United Methodist Church that Sunday morning. I had been invited to "join the church."

At the time, I was distant with Daddy and ambiguous about my feelings concerning him. Now thirteen years old, I was longing to be Daddy's "little girl" again. To be the apple of his eye. Yet too angry and confused to tell him. And I'd convinced myself that I was tougher now. Tougher in the sense that I didn't need anyone.

On the morning I joined the church, I was serving as an acolyte, lighting the candles on the altar. According to our church's tradition, the acolyte sat on the first pew after lighting the altar candles—in the very front row. After the sermon was preached, the invitation to join the church was extended to the congregation. I fidgeted in my seat as the plea was made. I wasn't moved or influenced by the sermon because I hadn't been paying attention; something beyond my understanding was making it more and more uncomfortable for me to sit still. Suddenly, my emotions erupted. I sobbed uncontrollably. I held my head down, trying not to draw attention to myself. As much as I didn't want to cry, I just couldn't control the tears. I fought and fought the urge to go up to that altar. Finally, I could no longer resist. I answered the invitation to join the church. It felt as if some mysterious force were compelling me. I couldn't explain it, but there I was at the altar.

Monica M. Johnson

Standing next to the pastor, drenched in tears, in plain view of the congregation, I felt no shame or embarrassment, as I'd feared I would. The ministerial staff greeted me with hugs and expressions of joy. I had been sitting in the church for years and had never responded to the call.

I sensed a change occurring within me. I'm not sure how or what was happening, but I felt different. The same force that had drawn me to the altar was making me feel as though somebody was going to listen to me—and care about me. I felt lighter. My heart no longer felt like a heavy rock within my chest.

I left the service hopeful that this moment would mark real change for me. The following Sunday, I attended the church's discipleship class as instructed. I was the youngest person there, and felt extremely intimidated. I didn't know the books of the Bible. I'd heard only Sunday-school stories. I was told that I was "born again" and Jesus loved me. Then the teacher read passages from the Bible, and the discussion afterward was boring and impossible for me to understand. I remember waiting for something to be said about what I'd experienced the previous Sunday. I was waiting for someone to embrace me, to make me better, and to reassure me that this good feeling wouldn't go away. Yet, there was nothing. I left the class feeling discouraged and unsure of myself once again. I was unclear about what was allowing me to feel peaceful while my situation was so horrible. I didn't know if the feeling would fade. I didn't understand what it meant to be loved by Jesus or to be born again. I was called a Christian, but no one, including Mama and my siblings, had explained what that title meant for me personally. Another Sunday passed and still I had no understanding. In class, we discussed the things we were required to do to get into Heaven. I was told not to cuss, not to smoke, and not to have sex before marriage, to name a few things. But the change that I'd experienced from within was like a vapor. Almost daily, I revisited the thought that I was a fool to believe in peace and happiness. I tried to accept the promises of a good future according to the Bible. I tried to believe in Jesus' love. But my brief moment of hope began to slip out of my reach. It seemed that the church had forgotten about me. No one followed up on my experience. As a result, I reached backward to hold onto Mama's belief in God and to live on her and Vanessa's prayers and faith. Soon, I couldn't even do that.

I was a teenager longing for purpose and longing for love. An introvert, I lacked the skills to socialize with others or to draw others to me. I decided I needed to make some changes to become someone likable. I tried a new, more up-to-date hairstyle. I started wearing clothing that fit my body and showed off my curves. I thought about dating, drinking, drugs, and sex. I had to consider all the things that would possibly allow me to fit in. Approval from adults was no longer my concern. Now, I wanted to be accepted among my peers. I had to stop acting like a child and grow up. The altar-call experience hadn't given me any direction or eased the pain of my childhood. I didn't know what was right or how to get the answers to my questions. So I began following what I was seeing in the world around me. I imitated those who didn't outwardly proclaim to be a Christian—the people who seemed happy because of the things they bought and the relationships they bounced in and out of.

Perhaps there was a God who had a purpose for my life, but I didn't know how to get to him.

A New Path

The altar-call feeling of being cleansed and renewed had given way to a horrible reality: I was back to being the person I wanted to forget. The weight that had been removed from my heart was back, and this time, there was an accompanying emptiness. I felt more alone, more worthless, more desperate, and more hateful than before.

It wasn't long before my increasing sense of loneliness led me to make foolish life decisions. I was sixteen years old and barely making it through high school. By my senior year, I was in great pursuit of finding happiness—and in grave danger of failing. As far as I was concerned, even if Daddy embraced me again, it was too late. I didn't want to be the apple of his eye. I no longer trusted in him. My childhood had left me bitter, not only toward my earthly father but also toward Mama's Heavenly Father. I felt that God had abandoned me a long time ago. It was too late for Him to enter my life, just as it was too late for Daddy.

All through my childhood I'd been told how much God loved me, and to trust Him. Yet, He never seemed to show up. I didn't trust Him to keep a promise. The years of seeing Daddy's drinking, of seeing that we didn't always have the best of things, and of seeing Mama being strong and sad was more than enough for me. I wanted out of this whole God thing.

For as long as I could remember, Mama had told us to pray and call on God because He was always listening. It seemed to me He wasn't listening at all, nor was He present. I didn't know how to identify Him in my negative situations. Mama said to thank God for everything. I couldn't figure out why I would want to thank God for the bad things that happened. Or why a good and loving God would allow these bad things to happen to us in the first place.

I had asked God to make me a better person. That didn't happen. I had pleaded with Him to make things around me better. Everything remained the same. I had believed and waited long enough. For the past eight years, I had believed that God could change my life, but he was taking entirely too long. I had lost the faith in the God that my great-grandma, grandma, and mama held fast to.

Mama had strong beliefs about how to live on Earth and get into Heaven. She taught firmly that we weren't supposed to fit in with the people in the world who didn't believe in our God. She was serious about avoiding drunkenness, foul language, and hating others. She told us over and over again about being nice to people who weren't nice to us. She taught us to love mean people, and to always forgive those who had harmed us. She talked all the time about doing the right thing, about being grateful for what little we had, and about not complaining. Mama said it was important to live a life that was pleasing to God. Mama remained faithful to God, but I couldn't see God's faithfulness toward her, considering the abuse she'd endured from Daddy and all of her struggles just to make ends meet. So I took God out of my plans.

I prayed occasionally, mainly for others, but I no longer wanted to use God as the center of my life. I wasn't able to see God as a real entity, as Mama said He was. I couldn't see Him as a being that was strong enough to control my little world, let alone the universe. How could He possibly hear and answer the prayers of so many? God was silent, leaving me to feel as if life "just happened."

It was time for me to try something new.

The search for my identity and for fulfillment continued. Daddy's drinking had made me hate the smell of strong liquor, but I began to drink alcoholic fruit drinks. I introduced myself to wine coolers, which seemed harmless and non-addictive. I drank them occasionally when I was alone, a few times a month. Eventually I became comfortable enough to try a mixed drink: a Fuzzy Naval. It was sweet and fruity like a wine cooler, and it became my drink. It was the one that "did it for me," made me feel relaxed. It contained more alcohol than the wine coolers, and I'd drink it on weekends.

Monica M. Johnson

My oldest sister, Carmen, frequently had get-togethers at her apartment. She'd invite her friends and we'd have drinks and play board games. I didn't have many friends, so I never invited anyone to come with me, but I enjoyed spending time with her friends, who were all older than I was by at least five or six years. Drinking with them made me feel accepted. Initially, I couldn't drink more than one six-ounce glass without feeling a little light-headed. After several weekends, I was able to drink more. I never knew what my limit was, but after I hit it, I'd come out of my quiet shell and become silly. I'd laugh at everything and anything. Occasionally, I'd feel promiscuous. Wanting to avoid that road, though, I'd just go to sleep.

While I was testing the waters of alcohol, Daddy enrolled in a twelve-step program to stop drinking. Mama felt that God had answered her years of praying for Daddy's drinking to end. Without notice or discussion, Daddy was gone into a rehab that required him to live in their facility. My siblings had all moved out by this point. Carmen lived nearby. Charles Jr. did as well, with his wife and son. Nan was enrolled in the navy and living in Virginia. Vanessa was attending college in Bowie, MD, about forty minutes away. She was the only one of my siblings aware of Daddy's difficult and long-awaited decision to get help. She was supportive and excited for him. Through her understanding of alcoholism, she saw Daddy's condition as a disease and had compassion for him. Vanessa forgave Daddy for the pain he'd caused during her childhood. I don't know if my other siblings forgave him or if they simply moved on, but the disappointment and anger within my heart wouldn't allow me to be happy about Daddy's steps toward rehabilitation. Whatever good I had felt at that altar two years ago was completely gone. And now with Daddy gone, I was feeling a whole new set of emotions involving my independence that I couldn't quite make sense of.

A few weeks had passed allowing Daddy to complete the initial phase of his rehab. Now he was able to invite the family to attend his group meetings. When I went to one of Daddy's Alcoholics Anonymous meetings, for the first time in years I looked into the eyes of "my daddy." I saw the man I once loved wholeheartedly, and the man who had returned that love. On his face, I saw peace—perhaps he felt free of the burden of his addiction. Deep inside, I wanted to give him another chance and love him. But I didn't know how to. Mama and Vanessa received him with open arms. They didn't relive or bring up his past mistakes. Or their anger. But I couldn't let go of mine.

I couldn't look past what his drinking and what his hurtful words and actions had done to me. I didn't have the strength to love him again. I was worn out from the nights I'd stayed awake worrying, the years of stomachaches and anxiety, and the tears of hopelessness and loneliness. I didn't have the mental equipment to respond to life's difficulties maturely. It seemed as if I were stuck at the age when the pain and disappointment were most intense. My reasoning was like that of a frightened child. Who was going to tell me how to overcome, how to get over it and move on as a balanced, loving adult without resentment?

Daddy was away for what seemed like forever but in reality was a month or so. While he was away, the house felt still, almost without walls. It felt open and safe. As a family, we didn't talk about Daddy being away, or when he would return. Our home and hearts had time to quiet down. Since I hadn't been communicating much with Daddy outside of showing hostility, I didn't miss having him there. I was free to try to figure out what these new emotions, ranging from curiosity to enthusiasm regarding my independence were really about. I would drink on occasion, but it was no longer satisfying. I was empty again. I needed something more in my life but had no clue what was missing. I felt ready for a relationship.

Monica M. Johnson

The Wrong Attention

For my first two years of high school (tenth and eleventh grade), I wasn't allowed to go to parties—Daddy was strict. But during my senior year, things changed. I started going out with my cousin. We hung out at the local roller skating parties but would always meet our curfews, to avoid being punished the following weekend. My curfew was earlier than hers but she was always willing to leave early with me.

One evening while she and I were hanging out at the mall, one of our favorite pastimes, I met the man who would become my first real boyfriend. Buddy was five years older, handsome, funny, and witty—and a bad boy. He was always into something that wasn't "on the up and up." But I liked him.

I had no idea how to be in a relationship but somehow, it had happened. I, Monica, the black sheep, had a boyfriend. A boyfriend my parents disapproved of. They quickly brought to my attention that he was too old for me—I'm fairly certain they meant he was too experienced sexually—so Buddy and I dated secretly. I felt he was the best thing for my life and that my parents were just being overprotective. We saw each other daily. He'd pick me up from school and drop me off without my parents seeing us. We'd also meet at the skate parties or the mall.

For a few hours on the week-nights, I was allowed to hang out with my girlfriend and more on the weekends. Often, I'd secretly meet with Buddy. We'd drive around, eat at fast-food restaurants, and hang out in parking lots. It wasn't long before the talking and laughing turned into touching and hugging.

My time with him never felt long enough. Initially, I kept my curfew faithfully. Since Daddy was away getting help for his drinking problem, Mama was left to enforce my curfew. Many nights, she was already in bed fast asleep when I returned. Unlike Daddy, who wanted everyone and everything shut down in the house before he went to bed, Mama trusted me to return as instructed. And so I started taking advantage of Mama's being asleep when I returned and extended my curfew to the early morning

Before long, I had trouble getting up for school and completing assignments for class. Barely making the grades, I began to slack even more. School wasn't a priority; finding happiness with my new boyfriend was. Sometimes I'd even skip school altogether. The phone call from my English teacher proved to be the wake-up call. She informed Mama and me that I wouldn't graduate if I didn't pull up my English grade. Terror consumed me. I had no idea how to study or improve my grades. I had no idea if I could do it in time to graduate.

But, with Mama's reprimand and my boyfriend's encouragement, I buckled down to get the job done. I stopped skipping class, did the work required, and still found time to spend with Buddy. When the school year was drawing to a close, I ordered my graduation cap and gown in the hopes that I'd be on the roster.

Senior prom was a highlight of this time. For some odd reason, Mama allowed me to attend with Buddy. I was so excited to finally be with him openly. And the good news continued. To my surprise, I discovered I'd earned the credits needed for graduation. Buddy and I celebrated as we planned a future together. He was already working as a truck driver as I planned to attend the local college.

Monica M. Johnson

Immediately after graduation, I visited Nan in Norfolk, VA. I'd planned to spend a few weeks with her before going to college in the fall. But a few days into my visit, I suddenly became ill. I couldn't eat without vomiting. Early morning was the worst, but I was sick all day, every day. Unable to figure out what was wrong with me, my sister and I called Mama and explained what was happening. "Put her on a flight back home," Mama told Nan. Unknown to us, Mama was keenly aware of what was "wrong with me."

I was pregnant.

I insisted she was wrong because *most* of the time I'd used protection—and teenage pregnancy wasn't going to happen to me. But I returned home as instructed, nervous about my condition. I'd never felt this way before and didn't know what could be the matter. The next day, Mama drove me to the doctor's office. The drive was quiet.

After signing in, I was immediately taken into the examination room. Mama stayed behind in the waiting room. Without looking back, I slowly proceeded down the hall, slightly bent over, my hands gently grasping my stomach. My exam consisted of a series of questions concerning my symptoms (vomiting, fatigue, nausea, weight loss, and no appetite), how long I'd had them, when the first day of my last menstrual cycle was, and so on. Totally unaware of the symptoms of first-term pregnancy, I anxiously hoped they could treat me with medication and get me feeling better immediately. Finally, I was excused to provide a urine sample.

Afterward, I returned to the exam room and waited, alone and nervous. What felt like hours (but was only a few minutes) later, my doctor tapped on the door. He stood tall in his white lab coat looking serious as he closed the door behind him.

Without delay, he spoke the words that dumbfounded me. "You're pregnant."

Tears immediately filled my eyes. We had a brief conversation about my options, and then an appointment was set for me to abort the pregnancy. The doctor released me to return to Mama, who had been given the news prior to the doctor's informing me. We were given information about a local clinic that would assist me in terminating the pregnancy. And that's all that was said about it.

I cried the whole way home. Because I had no idea what terminating the pregnancy involved, my focus was on the disappointment I'd caused Mama. Withholding the urge to bellow, I moaned and moaned. I attempted to control the erupting emotions by pressing tissues into my face. At one point, I had to ask Mama to pull over so I could vomit. I could hardly hold my head up because of the shame. I needed my mother to comfort me. Lacking the courage to ask, I felt as if I'd regressed to being a child again—I was a little girl, totally helpless but carrying a life within her. It was a grave reality.

A Path of Confusion

When the day came, no one knew about my pregnancy except Mama and Carmen. Upon arriving at the clinic, I experienced a major meltdown. Crying uncontrollably and hyperventilating before I could sign the consent papers, I was ushered out of the clinic by Mama and Carmen.

Aborting the baby was no longer an option, but it wasn't clear to me what this meant for my future. I was seven months shy of possibly becoming a mother. With the fetus inside me, I realized I wasn't nearly as grown-up as I'd thought I was. I didn't have all the answers to life—I didn't even know what was best for my life. But Mama never yelled, fussed, or even lectured me.

Monica M. Johnson

I decided to continue with my plans to go to college. I talked to Carmen, who was single and had a well-paying job, about taking the baby once it was born, and she agreed to raise the child as her own. Meanwhile, I had no idea how to tell Buddy that I wasn't sick at all but pregnant. And how was I going to tell him that I wasn't going to keep the baby? How would I explain that I wanted my sister to raise him or her? I also had to think about how to tell my dad. I had no idea how the news would affect him. What would it do to our already broken relationship? Then I worried about sharing the news with my sisters, especially Vanessa, the first to attend college. How was I going to tell them that their "baby" sister was expecting? Plus there was my granny, my great-granny, and Aunt Beverly, my "other mother."

I felt nauseous at the thought of facing everyone. It was too much to consider. The sadness was overwhelming. How had I gotten myself into this situation and how was I to move forward? The happiness of graduation, a new boyfriend, and plans for college had given way to a path of confusion, pain, and shame.

It wasn't until the end of the first trimester that the truth was exposed to my sisters. I wondered if Mama's silence was her way of dealing with the situation. Perhaps it was her way of allowing me time to deal with it in my own way. But for the most part, the silence felt like our way of pretending the issue didn't exist.

Once people knew, everyone tiptoed around the issue, mainly saying nothing, at least not to me. Following suit, I didn't sit anyone down to inform them of my pregnancy except my boyfriend and my daddy. Not talking to my sisters about the pregnancy was fine with me. And as a result of my avoidance, my sisters never talked to me about their true feelings about my pregnancy. I was okay with that as well. Buddy and I continued to date, as he too didn't share how he felt about the pregnancy. His continual involvement in my life was our way of moving forward.

By this point, Daddy had completed the twelve-step program. Along with the silence about my pregnancy, there was now also a silence about Daddy's recovery. We never discussed his experience, what it meant to us as a family, or how to move forward.

He was clearly different, though—he was quiet, settled, and not as uptight. I was different as well. I was no longer feeling the hatred toward him I'd felt before. Instead, I felt a warmth in my heart for him, but I had no idea how to put it into words. Deep inside, I wanted Daddy back in my life. I wanted us to be connected in a positive way.

He appeared to be somewhat sad, or possibly remorseful. And his quietness embraced me in a way that made me forget about the past pain. His sereneness made me dread all the more what came next: disappointing him with the news of my pregnancy.

Daddy's Little Girl

My knock on Daddy's bedroom door was gentle and could easily have been mistaken as a knock on the adjacent bedroom door. Part of me hoped he wouldn't hear it. Then I could put this conversation off for another time or another day. But he calmly said, "Come in."

It had been a long time since I'd heard my "old" daddy's voice— that voice that told me everything was okay. That voice that taught me life lessons. That voice that said I was his and he was mine. Today, I heard it.

My heart raced as I drew in a deep breath and hesitantly opened the door. Daddy was sitting on the edge of his bed. He often sat alone on his bed, and sometimes even in his car while parked in the driveway. He greeted me with the look that I also remembered from childhood—the look that said I was Daddy's little girl. With my head held low, I took a half step toward him and asked if we could talk. He nodded and gestured for me to come closer. I was certain my words would catch him off guard. I closed the door behind me and just blurted it out.

Monica M. Johnson

"Dad, I'm pregnant."

He took what seemed to be a nanosecond to collect his thoughts. Surely he felt a sense of disappointment? But that's not the message he conveyed to me. Even if it was what he felt, disappointment never showed on his face or in his voice. He reassured me that it wasn't the worst thing that could happen to me. He was in no way celebrating my pregnancy, but he was ready to help me move forward toward a successful future. In my pain and shame, I could feel my daddy still loved me and wanted to protect me. His response made me feel like I wanted to be reconnected to him.

I wondered if I could ever make him proud—truly proud, as I could no longer be his little girl.

A Baby Having a Baby

I pulled through the first and second trimesters wearing large sweatshirts to conceal my pregnancy. The baby was growing well, and so was I. Buddy and I were still dating, but I spent most of my time away from him. I had enrolled full-time in the local junior college and was working part-time at a hair salon. Unfortunately, my studies often suffered. I was always mentally exhausted worrying about what others thought about my pregnancy, and my need to nap often interfered with my study time. I barely had enough energy to get through the day. My grades were so low in the classes which I managed to maintain, that I was in jeopardy of losing my financial aid for the next semester.

When the fall semester ended, I was just three months away from my expected delivery date. The Christmas holiday was at hand. I was relieved to not have to go out in public, as my belly was difficult to hide at this point.

One day, while Mama and I rummaged through a bag of Christmas ornaments, in the midst of decorating the house, Buddy took the opportunity to "pop the question." He pulled a small box out of his pocket and presented a diamond ring. Dropping the ornament that was in my hand, I accepted the ring with much delight and shock.

Mama was clearly surprised, and Buddy and I felt her silence. Finally, she spoke. She asked Buddy several questions about what the ring meant and if he was ready to commit to both me and the baby. The conversation was short and to the point: he was going to marry me. Nothing more was said, and Mama and I continued decorating.

A wedding date was never discussed. But having a ring without a wedding date was fine with me. In my immature state, I didn't expect anything more.

A few weeks later, my due date was at hand. My best friend Carla and I were at the Annapolis Mall when I went into labor. In my ignorance, I brushed the contractions off as feeling "cramped" from walking too much. Taking frequent breaks, we kept wandering around the mall for another hour or so. Finally, unable to make sense of what was happening, Carla and I returned home so that I could rest.

Soon, the "cramping" became more intense and more frequent. It was Mama who informed us that I was in labor. So Carla and I began timing the contractions. She started the clock when I began to get short of breath and stopped it when I appeared to relax again. Initially, the cramps came every fifteen to twenty minutes, and then they were five minutes apart. "Carmen's baby" was on the way.

After an hour of intense pain and shortness of breath, it was time to go. Mama drove us to the hospital, and Carla comforted me through each contraction. At the hospital, some nurses quickly got me settled into a small room. I was told that I would be transferred to the delivery room—a room specifically set up to allow me to watch the birth through mirrors.

Monica M. Johnson

Hour upon hour, the pain would not let up. The nurses encouraged me to walk to speed up the process, but then the pain became so intense that I couldn't even do that. Mama phoned Buddy. Within the hour, he arrived. As the labor continued into its twelfth hour, Buddy sat at the edge of his seat, unsure of what to do.

Finally, the doctors decided to administer an epidural to relieve the pain, and that's when Buddy could no longer remain in the room. With tears in his eyes, he rushed into the hallway. He not only left the room but the hospital altogether.

A grueling fifteen hours after my labor had begun, we told Carla to go home. She was clearly exhausted and disturbed about my condition. Mama continued to sit with me as the doctors decided on the next course of action.

At hour twenty-four, without explanation I remained in the small room. Buddy had returned. It was finally time to push. And somehow, through my extreme exhaustion, I pushed out into the world a beautiful baby boy of five pounds. He was still and blue. Something was dreadfully wrong. The doctor worked hastily to remove the entangled nineteen inches of umbilical cord from around his precious tiny neck. The cord was removed but still there were no sounds. He appeared lifeless.

As my newborn was transferred from one hand to another, the attempt to revive him looked grim. Something thick, viscous, and dark was being aspirated from his fragile throat. No one would tell us what was happening.

I was petrified.

And then, finally, came the sound that every new parent yearns to hear: a resounding cry. He was alive, but to what degree? I wondered. Had he suffered some type of damage from the lack of oxygen? Fear gripped my heart. From across the room, the nurses reassured me that he was going to be okay. As they measured him, weighed him, and swaddled him, it was decided he needed additional care. I was able to kiss him just before he was whisked to neonatal care for closer observation.

My emotional ties wouldn't allow me to give him up to my sister just yet. He was diagnosed with jaundice, and I felt compelled to love him and keep him close to me. Carmen was able to hold him, but Buddy and I said nothing about her raising him. We named him Walter Joaquim III (Lil Walter). My newborn would prove to be strong and resilient.

Since Carmen spent much of her time at Mama's which meant her raising him would give me the opportunity to see him daily, with the money I'd earned working at the hair salon, I'd created a beautiful nursery in the spare room at Mama's house. Soft blues, whites, and yellows complemented the rocking horse décor throughout the room. And so, when Lil Walter was discharged, we were ready to receive him. Mama, Daddy, and I lived in the house now. Even though Buddy and I were parents, Daddy didn't allow him to stay overnight.

My strong bond with Lil Walter overshadowed my past guilt and shame, making it easy to love him openly. I was unable to separate myself from him. Giving up the baby to my sister was no longer a consideration. Carmen seemed to be okay with my decision. If she wasn't, I was unaware of her disappointment. We stopped bringing the issue up and just moved forward. She helped me care for him, and we developed a good system.

But it wasn't long before things went horribly wrong at the house. It seemed the good changes Daddy had undergone in the twelve-step program weren't enough to keep him and Mama together. Neither of them said a word about what was happening; all I knew was that Daddy was gone again. Once more, I remained silent. Silence was always the expectation. Mama and Daddy's split wasn't amicable by any means. Their fighting about the house, tools, furniture, and money became too much for me. My anger grew. And again, I blamed Daddy for leaving us.

Monica M. Johnson

Eighteen months after I gave birth to Lil Walt, Buddy and I were in a bad place in our relationship as well. Buddy appeared more stressed out, and began acting out of character. He wasn't patient or attentive to our needs, as he had been in the past. He became angry, uptight, and distracted by other issues in his life. Soon we were arguing more and I was spending an incredible amount of time being suspicious about his fidelity.

The day our arguing escalated into a physical confrontation, I told Buddy it was over. I was done being his girlfriend, or "fiancée." I was angry, hurt, confused, bitter, and frustrated. He'd gotten involved with some things that made me want to stay far away from him and his new lifestyle.

A New Creation

The breakup with Lil Walt's father had my head in a whirlwind. On the day of my next routine doctor's visit, my mind was everywhere but on the visit. I was present only physically.

I had no idea what was about to happen to me.

After taking my vitals and seating me in the exam room, the nurse informed me that the doctor would be with me shortly and left the room. I stared at the walls and read the charts and posters over and over to pass the time. I hated this part—the wait. Finally, I heard the long-anticipated tap on the door. When the doctor entered, I immediately noticed the concerned look on his face. There was no time to ask questions.

The doctor quickly launched into an explanation of what had been found during my last test and gynecological examination: abnormal cells. A biopsy was necessary. For now, I could go home. The thought that I might be dying briefly crossed my mind. I sat there alone, crying. Finally, unable to remain on the exam table forever, I got dressed and left the building. Driving home, I gathered my thoughts, considering the "what if it's cancer?" question.

When I reached Mama's house, I sat outside on the concrete steps and tried to work through the mounds of fears and questions in my mind. What would happen to Lil Walt if I died? What happened after this life, after death?

Suddenly, a realization hit me. I needed help. But not just any help. I needed spiritual help. I needed help from a power greater than myself. I needed God. I felt far from Him. Maybe because I spent no time thinking about Him in my daily routine? Maybe because I felt I didn't know how to pray? Maybe because I actually didn't know how to pray? I didn't spend much time at church anymore and knew very little about God. I wasn't sure why I was feeling this way now, but I was certain that I needed Him. I needed to find out how to get to Him. I needed God and others in my life to overcome this ordeal.

Tears fell steadily down my face. Though I felt hopeless and alone, I was simultaneously feeling something strange happening inside of me. It was the same warm, comforting feeling I'd had when I was thirteen years old and mysteriously "led" to the altar at my family church. Instantly, I knew God had heard my cry. I felt as if I would be okay and that I was safe from harm.

I wanted so much for God to heal me somehow. I didn't want to live in constant fear any longer, nor did I want to die. Before rising from the step, I cried out toward the sky, "If you heal me, God, I will live for you. I will believe in you and learn how to live for you.

Days later, after the biopsy, I returned to my doctor's office to get the results and possibly schedule surgery. But something shocking had happened—something extraordinary. The doctor told me the precancer cells were nowhere to be found. Examining me, he said he was also unable to find the area of the recent biopsy. There was no scar or evidence of it. He said he was pleased with how well I'd healed, and he appeared slightly stunned. I was stunned too. When I'd asked God to heal me, I hadn't known I could be healed so completely. I'd known nothing about miracles or the true power of prayer.

Monica M. Johnson

Gratitude flooded me. For the first time, I found myself extending my arms and hands toward the sky, as if I were waving to God and thanking Him for the miracles of hope and healing. I immediately went home, got on my knees, and thanked God again. I promised that I'd learn more about Him. Then I asked Him to show me how to live a life that pleased Him.

This time, I knew I had to take responsibility if I wanted to see a change in my life. I was responsible for doing something different in order to get different results. Inside, I was free. In my innermost being, I felt hope. There was no wondering if my life could become better. I didn't question whether I'd learn to live this faith thing, nor did I question whether God was with me. I had this inner reassurance that I was coming out of my vicious cycle of defeat. This time, I wouldn't hold others responsible—I would get to God myself.

Weeks passed, and I continued to walk faithfully with the vows I'd made to God, but not without struggle. The dark voices and the negativity continued to war against my desire to do well. In negative situations, I'd often return to the old thought patterns instead of seeing the best. I'd soon learn through the teachings of the church that this inner warring was referred to as "spiritual warfare" or the "enemy," and it was my job to learn how to overcome this force. I would need to "take authority" over it. To take authority meant doing something other than focusing night and day on the thoughts of despair and fear. I could not simply give up and die. I had to spend much more time thinking about the positives. I had to spend much more time sharing my thoughts with God and praying to Him for inner strength and wisdom. I had to behave in a way that indicated I believed something better was coming. I had to believe in God's power. I had to stop giving up and giving in to the fears.

I knew it was important for me not to look for help in anything or anyone outside of God. I knew that continuing to pray, envisioning my end result, and connecting with a church that would empower and restore me was the key to returning to God.

4. Listen to Your Father

Now choose life, so that you and your children may live and that you may love the LORD your God, listen to His voice, and hold fast to Him. For the LORD is your life. (Deuteronomy 30:19b–20a, NIV).

A New Experience

Returning to God and the things of God (i.e., prayer, the Bible, and meditation) renewed my inner being. The feelings deep within my heart and on the surface of my mind all seemed new. For the first time in years, I felt victorious over the negative thoughts. I felt joyful.

I reexamined my past and the choices I'd made that hadn't worked for my greatest good. I asked God for insight on what was keeping me from knowing Him on a deeper level. I no longer wanted to do things the way I had in the past. After all, when trouble had really hit my life, I'd struggled to find a way out before choosing to call on God. I didn't want to waste any more time being unproductive, so I included God in every part of my life. I prayed for guidance about what I should eat—it was important to me to be mindful of what I put into my physical body. I prayed for guidance about what to wear. I prayed for guidance concerning what church to attend and how to remain close to God. And most importantly, I prayed for guidance on how to hear from God.

I began attending church regularly. The church in which I'd grown up, well, it just didn't "feel" right any longer. In the same week I began praying to find a new church home, my cousin Carol invited me to see an incredibly uplifting, life-changing Christian play at a small church in Brandywine, MD. The play

Monica M. Johnson

was called *Girlfriend Boyfriend Thang*, and it depicted how we become consumed with the cares of life as young adults. It emphasized the issues, such as premarital sex and promiscuity, that surround girlfriend-boyfriend relationships and provided great insight. The performance displayed God's amazing ability to forgive us and pursue us and reveal to us purpose for living. Finally, it graciously invited us into a loving relationship with God, our Creator, Lord, Father, and friend. My heart was wide open to receive more of Him.

After the play, the pastor gave a brief talk on God's spirit—the Holy Spirit. He enlightened us on how God is more than an unseen God. I'd never heard such a teaching before. I sensed myself opening to a greater awareness of God's being. The atmosphere within the small sanctuary was charged with power and excitement. I felt hope and love beyond words and beyond measure.

Then the pastor asked people to join him at the altar. He invited those who didn't know God and who, like me, had turned away from God to come forward to connect or reconnect with God. He requested that those who needed a church home, a place to worship, and a place to learn the Bible come forward to join his church. It was amazing. The same unseen force that had led me to the altar when I was thirteen and the same presence that had comforted me after I received the dreadful news at the doctor's office was present again, here in this room.

"The Holy Spirit is urging you to come forward," the pastor said. The experience was spiritual. It was the Holy Spirit that had been the positive, powerful force with me all along. Now I had a name for it, or Him. The pastor explained that the Holy Spirit was the spirit of God, or the breath of God. I found myself being led to the altar once again. I had remained in my seat during the initial plea because I doubted the need. After all, I'd already done this before, so why again? But as I asked the questions in my mind, the pastor would speak the answers, as if he could hear my every thought. It was apparent that this Holy Spirit could hear my inner cries and concerns.

And so, I finally relinquished the fight and surrendered to the presence (the Holy Spirit). I stood at the altar with others who were possibly experiencing the Holy Spirit as well—some in ways that were strange and new to me. Some people were on their knees leaning over the altar. Some were weeping uncontrollably. Some were doing what appeared to be a dance of some kind. And some had their hands raised in the air as if they were waving to God—just as I'd done when I got the report that I was no longer ill. Then there were others who were standing in silence. I could only guess that we had all responded to God's nudging. God apparently spoke through this Holy Spirit, and I was able to sense Him, just as others could. And in my willingness to surrender to God's nudging, I could sense this was to be my new church home. I just felt that I was in the "right place." It fit me.

That night, while at the altar, I committed to joining the church.

As we were leaving, the pastor asked everyone to repeat after him. Then he said a prayer affirming the belief that Jesus is the Christ and that God raised Him from the dead. He also prayed that we would repent (recognize our wrongs or the things that turned us away from God) and surrender to the higher power, God the Heavenly Father. Acknowledging our sins was a beginning—a way to recognize that we had returned to God and been accepted by Him, and that our lives were now made new.

My new church, Gibbons United Methodist Church, was located about forty-five minutes away from where I lived. I traveled to this spirit-filled church two, sometimes three, times a week. Every Sunday yielded an atmosphere unlike anything I'd ever experienced in church before. I began to transform from a humdrum girl in a vicious cycle of defeat to a girl with a new zeal for life—a girl who loved and laughed. This character change was noticeable to others as well. Initially, friends and relatives challenged my decision to break tradition and leave the family church. However, just weeks after I faithfully began attending services at Gibbons, my mother and sisters would occasionally join me, only to experience for themselves the wonders I'd shared.

Monica M. Johnson

Eventually, the Holy Spirit led Carmen and Malissa to join the church as well. We learned how God speaks through the Holy Spirit, and of the power (works) of the Holy Spirit. We learned about prayer (talking and listening to God and learning the voice of God). We learned about the power of healing (physically, emotionally, and mentally). We learned about being freed of past pain that keeps us stuck and unproductive. We learned about faith and how to please God through faith. We learned about anointing with olive oil. The pastor would ask for God's blessing upon the oil and then anoint people or things with it. To be anointed was to be blessed by God through the hands of another. In being anointed with oil, the person or thing was consecrated (declared holy or dedicated for a specific use). On people, this consecration was done by rubbing or smearing the oil on part of the person's body, usually the head. Often it was done for healing, or as part of a religious ceremony, or to install somebody officially or ceremonially into a position or office.

My increasing spiritual knowledge empowered and renewed me daily, and this made me want to talk to God all the more. More importantly, I wanted to hear Him speak. I wanted so much to sense His presence with me daily. I realized more and more that hearing Him wasn't only possible but necessary to remain focused and spiritually strong.

My prayers used to feel like one-way communication. Amazingly, now I was able to talk to God and hear Him speak to me. His responses weren't always immediate, but I grew confident that they were sure to come and that my patience was a sign of trust in Him.

There was no one way that God spoke. Occasionally, it was an audible voice—I'd often wondered if that was even possible. I cannot explain it fully, but I heard Him just as clearly as if I were speaking to someone in person. Usually, though, he spoke to me through what I call a "still" voice. It allowed me to sense what was spoken. Sometimes, it was a case of "something told me…"

For example, I'd get this nudge telling me to take a specific route while driving. Then I'd later learn that there was bumper-to-bumper traffic on my normal route. I learned to count these "small" things as blessings, and doing so trained me to hear the greater things later.

There were times that audible voice allowed me to be a blessing to others. One Sunday morning, I was rushing out of the house to get to church. Right before I closed and locked the door to my apartment, something "told me" to go back inside to grab feminine products, which I had no need for at the time. Once I arrived at the church, I visited the restroom, where a young lady was frantically asking if anyone had feminine products. I was thrilled that I'd listened to the voice, as that "small" thing was a big blessing for that young lady.

And sometimes, I would feel an urge to call someone at a specific time, and I would end up calling them when they really needed encouragement or something else I could give them.

Yielding to the voice of God didn't mean I was never stuck in traffic, or that there were no adverse events in my life. Nor did it mean I did everything perfectly. Instead, yielding allowed me to handle situations with peace, confidence, and hope. It allowed me to see the lessons to be learned. Yielding gave me the option to lay down the negative thoughts and choose life. It taught me that each closed door, missed opportunity, trial, and disappointment had a purpose that wasn't always clear to me in the moment.

There were many other ways in which I heard God: through dreams; an unsettled feeling in my belly; words of knowledge from others; visions; songs; scriptures; television shows; others' life experiences; prophets/prophetesses; and the pastor on Sunday morning. I could hear Him more quickly and more clearly when I was silent—more specifically, when I silenced my thoughts and worries about a situation and tried not to figure out what steps to take. Silencing my thoughts allowed me to be open to His answer without a preconceived one getting in the way.

Monica M. Johnson

I could hear His voice at any time. I didn't have to be at an altar, or on my knees with my eyes closed. I could hear Him while I was working, playing, doing chores, hanging out with friends, praying, crying, singing, or simply enjoying time alone. Sometimes I heard "nothing"—though I received no instructions, I'd receive a settled mind and an ease within my spirit. And I'd know it was my time to "just wait." In those times, I didn't make any changes in my life. I would continue my daily routine and the answer would come later (in God's timing). Sometimes it would "fall in my lap" (in God's timing).

God is always speaking, and He is available when we call on Him. In the past, I'd thought that only church leaders or those who could speak in the prayer language ("tongues") could hear him. I was delighted to learn that He speaks to everyone, all the time—even when we aren't doing what's considered right. He is a loving God that cares about us.

The knowledge I gained about prayer and God's presence was enlightening and liberating. I couldn't imagine living without His guidance again. I was excited about my relationship with the Lord. I'd never thought I would get to know him this intimately. This kind of relationship was something that had seemed to happen only to others. For the first time, I felt like one with great favor.

Being in a relationship with God not only allowed me to see negative situations in a positive light, but it also allowed me to operate in ways that were victorious. For example, I learned that forgiving didn't have to involve forgetting. Forgetting a situation was nearly impossible for me, but in true forgiveness, I was able to remember what happened but no longer experience the hurt. Thus, the offense lost its power over me and over my responses. I was able to understand others and not condemn them for the wrong they might have inflicted on me. It was as if I could feel their pain and see into their misfortunes. I didn't justify misdoings, but now I could forgive instead of harvesting bitterness and hate.

In the process of forgiving, I was able to make peace in relationships where there had been division. More specifically, I was able to address the issues concerning my dad. And beyond the forgiveness, I began to feel compassion and love for the man I had vowed to hate throughout eternity. The love I'd had for my dad in the days when I'd sit on his lap was restored in my heart. I chose not to dwell on the bad things and to let go of the resentment, fear, and pain, and in doing so, I made room for love. Deep within my heart I felt a new sense of adoration for Daddy. I started smiling when he walked into the room.

The act of forgiving was therapeutic. It was incredibly pleasing to let go of things and move on with a positive attitude—move on without making the person who'd hurt me pay for what they'd done. As each opportunity to forgive arose, I confronted my past. I confronted each situation and person by first looking at my wrongdoing and then, when possible, I confronted the person with whom I was at odds. I didn't always receive an apology in return, nor did I get to address every issue of my past, but my heart felt clean. I felt ready to move forward and become more of the person God had created me to be—in other words, I felt ready to live purposefully.

My misconception that I had to physically do things to get into Heaven was put to rest as I gained an understanding of what it meant to be born again in a spiritual sense. I learned that following the lead of God's Holy Spirit, leading others into a relationship with God, and becoming a better person daily were some of the ways to God's heart. I was no longer responsible for living a perfect life. I could live joyfully in this world without feeling guilty about the things I might need to change along the way. It was not my job to please all people, but it was certainly my job to be at peace with my daily decisions.

Monica M. Johnson

Appointed to Serve

Two years had passed since my born again experience. During those two years I met PJ at Gibbons United Methodist church. In addition to attending church together occasionally we would hangout. PJ and I became close friends, I called him my brother. It was December 1994 when PJ, came by with a Christmas gift. PJ and I had a special friendship. We didn't get together often, but when we did, we talked openly and honestly. It was clear from the moment he arrived that this visit had a purpose. There was no joking or kidding around, as usual. Instead, he got straight to business, calling Lil Walter and me into the dining room. He held a large bottle of virgin olive oil in his left hand. Without saying a word, he picked up a chair in his right hand and placed it in the middle of the floor. Then he instructed me to take off my shoes and socks and sit on the chair. I did so willingly.

After explaining to Lil Walt, who was seven at the time, what the oil was for, PJ directed his attention back to me. He told me to bow my head and extend and cup my hands. As Walter stood watching curiously, PJ poured the oil onto my head. It gently flowed down, trickling onto my forehead and parts of my face. I bowed my head further, and the oil flowed into my cupped hands, through the cracks between my fingers, and finally onto my feet, which were directly beneath my hands.

It was clear that PJ was being used by God to anoint me for service. As God through PJ was setting me apart in this way, the Holy Spirit nudged PJ to read from the book of Samuel which explained how David had been anointed secretly as king and later it was done publicly much like what was happening to me. PJ explained how the anointing on David's head stood for holiness just as it represented holiness upon me.

Although I didn't fully understand the work ahead of me, I sensed this anointing was important and had purpose beyond my understanding. So without saying a word, as instructed, I reached out to hold Lil Walter's hands as PJ prayed for me and the work that I would eventually do for God.

"Alone"

In the weeks and months that followed the anointing, my days were extremely busy. I was attending two to three church services a week, ministering (encouraging with the scriptures/words of hope) on the phone to hurting women and girls at all hours of the night, and studying the Word (Bible scriptures) daily. I had been working at the hospital as a histopathology lab tech for the past three years while attending on-campus college classes, single-parenting, and spending time with my family and friends. Needless to say, I became physically exhausted. I wanted to help everyone who needed help, and foolishly, I didn't turn away anyone who asked. The good works that I was performing began to overwhelm me.

Despite my friendships and my time with family, I felt alone. In the hours I should have been asleep, I was filled with anxiety and worry about the things I had to complete. In the time I usually set aside to pray, I was either sleeping or unable to focus. I gave of myself to the church, to strangers, to family, and to work but I was frustrated and perplexed about my own life. My heart was full of everything but peace.

Surely God was present, but I could no longer hear Him or feel His presence.

Monica M. Johnson

5. The Raging Storm

I give you this instruction in keeping with the prophecies once made about you, so that by following them you may fight the good fight, holding on to faith and a good conscience. Some have rejected these and so have shipwrecked their faith. (1 Timothy 1:18–19, NIV)

The Storm Breaks

It was the fall of 1995, and I was tired. Worn out. Listening for the Father's voice. I felt as if the skies in my life were constantly overcast. Nothing serious, but dreary. My heart was heavy.

I'd just finished a shift at Anne Arundel Medical Center, and my coworker was trying to persuade me to have the blood-work portion of my yearly health exam done before I left. Even though I worked as a phlebotomist, I had a fear of needles. In fact, I was a complete coward about them. My coworker wanted to draw my blood, but I wouldn't be persuaded. I told him that I didn't have enough time because I was on my way to Mama's house. Lil Walt and my niece, Kylea, of whom I had temporary custody, would be waiting to see me before going to school. Conveniently, the hospital was only ten minutes from Mama's house. Seeing the kids in the morning and helping them get ready for school was a highlight of my day.

As usual, I called Mama to tell her that I was on my way and would see her in a few minutes. Then I said goodbye to my coworker. We laughed about his persistence and my fear of needles before I headed to my car.

This particular morning was extremely cold. The roads were patchy with something the meteorologists called black ice (which I wasn't familiar with)—ice that's thin and almost invisible.

Normally, the day-shift workers would mention something about the road conditions, but I hadn't heard anything about icy roads.

Five minutes into my travel, I approached the Severn River Bridge, which spans the Annapolis Naval Academy. There seemed to be some kind of film on it. I eased my foot onto the brake and squinted, unable to make sense of what I was or wasn't seeing.

I said to myself, "Is there something on the bri—?"

Before I completed the word, my car spun out of control.

Horrified, I felt as if I were moving in slow motion. I screamed out to God for help. My car veered into the opposite lane. Suddenly, seemingly out of nowhere, a car was rapidly approaching.

"Oh, God, please don't let me die like this! Oh, no! LORD! Please don't let me kill anyone!"

And then my world became quiet.

My car was demolished. My body shattered. Traffic quickly backed up on the bridge for miles and miles in both directions.

The solid steel frame of the oncoming car, an old Cadillac, had ripped through the driver's side of my little two-door and violently pushed the elements of the door into my body. To onlookers, it appeared as if the Cadillac's bumper had actually torn into my body. The busted steering wheel hung on my lap. Shattered glass covered the seats and dashboard. The rear window had exploded, leaving nothing but a bent frame. My face bled; the greatest laceration was at the left temple. Blood filled my mouth and dribbled down my lip as I made vain attempts to cry for help.

Monica M. Johnson

Onlookers rushed to the scene and called 911. My sister-in-law, Athena, was only one car away from my tragedy. She rose quickly and peered out the window of her car. Staring at the wreckage in fear, she questioned the identity of the car that resembled mine. With great trepidation, she got out of her vehicle. And then, heart racing and fear gripping her, she walked toward the wreckage only to see what she'd dreaded most.

In a panic, she abruptly turned away from the wreck and rushed back to her vehicle. To her, I appeared to be dead. Her friend, who was driving her vehicle, demanded she return to my side. Frantic and grief-stricken, she approached my car again. That's when she realized I was alive, but barely. I looked up at her and muttered that my stomach hurt.

Seeing the brokenness of my body and the pain in my cry for help was more than Athena could handle. She turned and walked away in despair again, but her friend persuaded her to return to my side once more.

Then Athena made the call that would change my family's life forever. Emergency vehicles were en route as Athena contacted Mama with the grim news.

The Storm Intensifies

Mama had been expecting me to walk in the door at any moment. Barely able to speak, Athena found the words to tell Mama that I had been in a horrible car accident on the nearby bridge and the outcome didn't look good.

In disbelief, Mama hung up the phone and took a moment to breathe and gather her thoughts. Lil Walt walked into the kitchen as Mama gasped for air. She didn't say a word. But Walter looked into Mama's eyes and said, "Something bad has happened to my mom?"

Then Kylea walked into the room. Mama told them that I'd been in a car accident. Without a second thought, she took their hands and began to pray. Moments later, she instructed Walter and Kylea to continue praying for me. Then Mama called her mother, who lived a few houses away, told her the news, and asked her to come to the house to stay with the children.

Unable to wait for Granny's arrival, Mama jumped into her car, rushed out of the driveway, and drove straight to Anne Arundel Medical Center. When Mama arrived at the local hospital, she was devastated to learn that I wasn't there. She informed the emergency-room receptionist of my accident and asked why I hadn't arrived. Unaware of my situation, the receptionist couldn't help her, and Mama came close to sheer panic.

Seeing a paramedic passing by, Mama demanded help from him. He took her by the hands and informed her that there had been several car accidents in the area and that he'd find out where I was. After consulting with other staff in the ER, he returned to inform Mama that I had been killed instantly in the crash.

Still in disbelief, Mama denied my death. She insisted he was wrong and demanded that he continue to inquire about my physical whereabouts. She gave the paramedic additional details about the location of my accident in hopes that he'd made a horrible mistake. Again, he consulted with other staff. The ER was buzzing with traumatic injuries, one after another, leaving little room for Mama to monopolize the staff's attention.

Finally, after relentless inquiring, the paramedic who was assisting Mama learned that the person who had died was not me. He apologized profusely for being misinformed and suggested Mama inquire with other staff to find my location. Feeling little relief, Mama addressed another paramedic nearby and was told that due to the number of accidents in the area, there were no vacant beds for patients in this hospital and that I'd been flown by helicopter to Prince George's Hospital, located just outside our county.

Monica M. Johnson

At this point Mama was no longer able to contain herself. She fell apart, crying hopelessly. She had no idea how to get to Prince George's, and no family was there to console her. Having been given no details of my condition, Mama was left to think the worst. She began talking aloud, telling herself that everything would be okay and searching the atmosphere for answers.

Realizing she needed to set her mind at ease in order to deal with what was ahead, she walked out of the ER and down the hallway, into the chapel. Meekly, she knelt down at the altar and pleaded to God for help and for understanding of my condition. As she prayed silently, the Lord began speaking to her in what she described as an audible voice that only she could hear. One by one, she began to call out my body parts that needed God's healing. Each time she heard God say an organ, she repeated it: "Colon, liver, kidneys, bladder, *lungs*."

When she heard nothing more, she ended her prayer by asking God to be with me. Her anxiety was eased and her need to cry was gone. She gained the strength to rise to her feet. Her fears silenced, she was able to return home and get directions to Prince George's Hospital.

My cousin Dale, my dad, and Vanessa were waiting anxiously at the house, having heard of the accident. Word of my collision had spread quickly. Upon Mama's safe arrival, they all piled into one vehicle and were on their way. By this time, the temperature had risen and the ice on the roads had melted. Silently, they headed quickly in what they thought was the right direction, but an hour later, they realized they were lost.

Battling to gain a sense of direction, they all became unglued. Another hour passed before they finally arrived.

The Strength to Hope

Much to their surprise, they entered the ER to find numerous familiar faces: close friends, other family members, and church staff. Their numbers filled the ER almost to capacity, creating an atmosphere of much-needed strength and hope. Mama took a deep breath in and then exhaled feeling a stillness. To mama, the familiar faces appeared as an angelic host that stood taller than the walls and as high as the ceilings, watching over and preparing my family for what was to come. For a moment, Mama simply stood in awe of the crowd that had gathered. The angelic presence gave Mama, Daddy, and Vanessa courage.

Still, nothing could have prepared them for what they were about to hear and see. A nurse gingerly motioned for them to follow her into an isolated area, where the surgeon met them.

There was no time to spare. The surgeon immediately informed them that the extent of my injuries wasn't fully known but I was losing a lot of blood and required surgery. Just as quickly as they would give me a unit of blood, I would lose it. He said he didn't know what to expect in surgery but that it was imperative. He needed to identify the internal injuries and stop the bleeding.

My family just shook their heads, feeling there was nothing more to say. Then the surgeon looked at them and said sternly but softly, "Two of you can go in to see her one last time."

The words "one last time" unleashed the unjust winds of this raging storm. Stricken with grief and barely able to stand, Mama attempted to walk into the room where I lay on a gurney. Vanessa and Daddy followed. The nurse stopped them: "Only two allowed into the room." But Vanessa refused to be left in the waiting room. She wanted to touch me and see me and nobody was going to stop her. And so it was.

Monica M. Johnson

As the three of them proceeded toward the room, Mama heard: "Do not focus on what she looks like." She heard these words repeatedly as she drew closer to me. Looking behind her, she saw no one. Mama knew that faith didn't require vision, yet vision could easily blur the faith of the believer.

> *Now Faith is being sure of what we hope for and certain of what we do not see.*
> *(Hebrews 11:1, NIV)*

My unconscious body appeared to be dead. Instantly, Vanessa broke down, wailing. Mama reached out to her as Daddy insisted that everyone be strong and not cry in front of me. He didn't want me to sense how serious my condition was. Lying upon the gurney was a body that had changed almost beyond recognition. I was connected to tubes and machines, my skin had darkened to a deep shade of black, my entire body was swollen, and my eyes were bulging beyond the sockets. I was badly broken.

Mama instantly went into a state of denial. Disputing that the body was mine, she begged to see her daughter. Daddy and Vanessa were close to Mama's side reassuring her of the gruesome truth. The surgeon quickly interjected and confirmed my identity. He informed them that the surgery would take at least six hours but could be longer.

The dreaded question was asked: "Is she going to make it?"

The surgeon drew in a breath and looked at my family. "Say your goodbyes, she may not make it. We will do all that we can for her."

The Fight of Faith

Mama planted her feet firmly on the floor to avoid giving in to her buckling knees. Her gaze swept my body, head to foot, foot to head, and she began to weep. Raising her hand to her chest, she held her heart as if it were literally breaking, and then raised cupped hands to her mouth to avoid wailing. While in my unconscious state, she touched my hands, reassuring me that she was there for me and everything would be okay. Tears dropped from her eyes as she did so. Daddy echoed Mama's words of comfort as he gently placed his hands upon my cold hand. Vanessa leaned on Daddy, losing her composure and wailing as Daddy had previously instructed her not to do.

Then I was hastily rolled away toward the operating room. No more touching. No more words to be spoken. Mama, Daddy, and Vanessa turned in a huddle and held one another for several minutes. Daddy released his grip first and ushered them into the waiting room, which was now overflowing with friends and family. Their expressions were sullen as Mama gravely informed them of my prognosis. Although the clock on the wall said it was daytime, it quickly became night in their hearts. It was a dark moment. The stars refused to shine.

They sat together, stood against the walls together, paced the floors together, and mostly hoped for the best together. Some meditated on Scripture, holding fast to the promise of a miracle. Some turned their faces to the wall in fervent prayer. Some sat quietly. And others danced a ceremonial dance of faith. They were all determined to remain faithful as they awaited the surgeon's return.

Monica M. Johnson

6. Raised Up!

Is any one of you sick? He should call the elders of the church to pray over him and anoint him with oil in the name of the Lord. And the prayer offered in faith will make the sick person well; the Lord will raise him up. The prayer of a righteous man is powerful and effective. (James 5:14–15a, 16b, NIV)

Against All Odds

The waiting room never became stagnant. There was hope. Prayers and praising filled the air. Still, anxiety occasionally worked its way into the spirit-filled atmosphere. Vanessa, who can usually be counted on to give an encouraging word in the worst of storms, headed to the hospital gift shop to find something to keep everyone occupied. She purchased a jigsaw puzzle of Peanuts characters: Snoopy, Charlie Brown, and a few others. The puzzle was filled with humor, life, and vibrant colors, and it gave my loved ones an outlet for their nervous energy. Everyone took turns adding a piece to the puzzle.

Then the surgeon returned—sooner than expected. Four hours had passed. He approached with reluctance, and his expression held little hope. First, he explained that he'd done all he could do to help me. Then, he told all gathered about the additional injuries discovered during surgery. My liver, colon, bladder, and kidneys were lacerated. My spleen had been removed. Worst of all, one of my lungs had collapsed during the surgery; as a result, they'd had to insert tubes in both lungs (the other lung had collapsed during the accident). I was now connected to a life-support machine (ventilator). Another surgeon was still rebuilding my shattered pelvis with pins, plates, and screws. The next twenty-four hours would be critical. The good news was that

I'd made it through the most difficult part of the surgery; the bad news was that there still wasn't much hope. There was nothing for anyone to do at this point except pray. The doctor suggested that everyone go home to rest. My loved ones left with great trepidation.

When dawn dissolved the night, what my family hoped had been a horrible nightmare was a reality. Still heavily sedated from the surgeries, I was barely hanging on. The machine breathed air into my almost-lifeless body. The staff didn't expect me to awaken or be responsive in any way. However, without notice, I woke.

Eyes wide open, I slowly scanned the room, attempting to make sense of my surroundings. Making eye contact with the attending nurse, I communicated my perplexity with a look of bewilderment accompanied by groans, gestures, and utterances. (In their absence, the nurse would share the series of events with Mama and Carmen upon their return). The stunned nurse quickly informed other staff of my alertness. Then, after explaining to me where I was and what had happened to me, the nurse telephoned my family to inform them of my unfathomable alertness. Mama answered on the first ring. The nurse warned her that I wasn't out of danger and my situation was still critical. Hearing only the good news, Mama hung up and shared it with the family.

The nurse would later tell Mama when they informed me that the family were on their way back to visit me, I attempted to communicate with her through fingerspelling, the manual alphabet used by people who are deaf. Unfortunately, the nurse didn't understand it, but once she realized that I had use of my right hand, she placed my fingers around a pen and a piece of paper towel before me. I ran the pen along the paper, and my scribbles contained one or two words, and parts of a word that phonetically made sense.

A short time later, my family arrived, renewed by a smidgen of relief and hope. They had asked God for a miracle and believed my unexpected alertness was their answer. Often misunderstood for their faith-walk, the family didn't allow the staff, who believed the celebration was premature, to steal their hope.

Monica M. Johnson

In my private room, Mama settled down on the chair next to my bed. Just before Mama's arrival, I had directed multiple questions to the nurse concerning my medical care. My questioning prompted the nurse to ask Mama if I was studying medicine. She explained that I worked in a hospital. Then the nurse handed Mama the paper, which was filled with instructions.

While Mama, Carmen, and the nurse were attempting to make sense of my scribbles, I gestured a need to communicate with Mama. The nurse remained at her side as Mama placed a pencil in my hand. I began to write. I told Mama that my body was in excruciating pain but that "my spirit was radically praising God." At that moment, Vanessa arrived. She cautiously entered the room and watched me wiggle my toes and fingers to show them how I was praising God. Their expressions of joy resounded throughout the room. The medical staff looked shocked by my alertness.

Then Mama grabbed several notes and cards that had been left in my room by visitors. She sat close to my side and read aloud the get-well wishes. I kept my eyes fixed on Mama as I faintly listened to the words of hope and encouragement. Focusing on reading the words, Mama didn't notice my strength weakening. She shared the messages from friends, family, coworkers, and even strangers—from people down the street and all the way to the west coast. Their letters articulated a deep longing for me to be healed. Their heartfelt cries stretched from the pages that Mama held so tightly. She later told me that while reading these messages, she felt a warmth and love that lifted her beyond her pain and worries. The warmth even increased the level of hope in the atmosphere around her.

Mama wasn't certain how much I was able to comprehend, but she sure gained hope from seeing me alert. After she'd read the last of the cards, I indicated that I wanted to communicate something. Writing on the paper towel that was still before me, I told Mama to let everyone know I needed their prayers. My gaze raced aimlessly about the room, as if I were searching for what they needed to pray for. Mama watched me intently.

I began to write again.

I asked that they wouldn't pray for God to take me out of my horrific situation but instead for God to give me the strength to endure to my end. Too weak to continue, I let my eyes close, and my breathing slowed. I began to drift in and out of sleep.

Mama quietly rose from her chair with the paper towel and walked out of my room, her head low. She leaned her forehead against a wall and prayed. "Lord God, I need strength. Give my baby the strength to endure. Please Lord God. Amen." She used both hands to push away from the wall. Then, her head still low, Mama returned to my room. Carefully, she placed the paper on the counter next to the chair beside my bed, and then she sat down, watching me slowly breathe. A tear dropped from her weary eye. Then she noticed my eyes open once more. She cautiously yet quickly leaned closer. Wiping the tear from her face, she stared at me, making sure not to break eye contact. I gestured nothing. My eyelids closed again.

Monica M. Johnson

My arm was resting at my side as I slightly lifted my index finger two times. Mama caught the ever-so-slight movement and grabbed the paper towel from the counter. She quickly positioned it in front of me and fixed my fingers around the pencil. She and Carmen, who had never left the room, anxiously awaited my message. My breathing was slow. I appeared to be perplexed, a frown wrinkling my brow. My eyes gazed into the atmosphere, searching for answers. No one said a word. The only sound was the ticking of the clock. Seconds went by. Then minutes. The pencil remained between my fingers and rested on the paper. Mama and Carmen never turned away. They waited. Quietly, they waited.

Finally, I looked down and wrote a question. When the words became legible, time stood still. Mama and Carmen froze, unable to respond. The lights, the sounds, the machines, the drips—everything was suspended in midair.

Why did you allow this to happen to me?

Nothing profound about this question. But it held power. Mama and Carmen had no answer, and spoke no words in a vain attempt to soothe me.

Then my hand lifted and my fingers began to move slowly across the paper towel again.

Who better to use than my child...

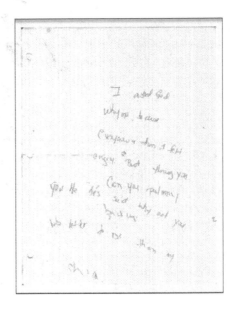

The pencil fell from my fingers. Instantly, light and sound returned to the room. The ventilator exhaled. The heart monitor's lights flashed and pulsed. Mama's and Carmen's hearts thumped. Their breath entered the air in waves. Life had returned to everyone... except me.

Realizing that something had shifted, Mama and Carmen focused on my face, which had gone blank. The noise of the machines slowed. Something was wrong. Carmen raced to find help.

Soon, nurses were scurrying about my room, making adjustments to the ventilator. I was no longer breathing on my own. I seemed to be drifting away. My question had been asked and the answer had been given. But what was next? Why had I been led to write the question and answer? What did it mean to be "used" by God? Was God suggesting this was the end? Death? Was He suggesting I was being used to show suffering? Had God Himself put this pain on me as judgment? Was it a mark of sin? Of shame? Of sin or shame in whom? Me? Others? Was He a cruel God? Was God still with me after all I'd been through? Was a miracle even possible?

Monica M. Johnson

Expecting a Miracle

Weeks went by. My communication had stopped. I was unresponsive. The longer I remained on the ventilator, the less likely my chances of recovery were. The dreaded question of "pulling the plug" hovered.

On a schedule, family members sat reading get-well wishes to a body they could only hope would once again respond to their voices. Day after day and night after night, cards were added to the wall, yet the medical reports yielded only greater dismay. Snowfall after snowfall, my loved ones made their way from home to hospital. Despite their fear and anxiety, nothing would stop them from believing in a miracle. They would touch my body with oil and sing it songs.

A special note was taped just outside the entrance to my room:

> *Do not enter if you are negative or doubtful about Monica's healing. Please read the scriptures and play healing music during your visit.*

A CD player sat on the counter. A CD of Pastor Kenneth Copeland was available for the staff to play for me if the weather prevented the family from making it to the hospital. When they did visit, the family became "authorities" over my body. Mama often whispered directly and passionately to it, commanding my lungs to function on their own, commanding my blood to be cleansed of any disease, commanding my bones to go back into place and for my body to heal without complications. Sometimes she'd rub my entire body from head to toe with olive oil, anointing it.

There were others who visited daily and lay their hands upon my body, and on one occasion, my cousin Debbie lay her entire body over me. Her covering my body was a way of transferring life back to me. My loved ones were determined not to allow any negativity to rest in their minds and hearts—negativity that would cause them to forget about a miracle.

The sounds of the ventilator keeping me alive echoed constantly. It made both high-pitched and low-pitched noises, and they were accompanied by bright lines that bounced up and down the monitor. Tubes were connected to every part of my body, and bags of fluid dripped into me through intravenous lines. A tube in my throat passed air to my lungs and connected me to the ventilator. A filter in my inferior vena cava prevented blood clots, and tubes in my chest cavity aided my breathing further.

There were plates and screws in my pelvis to replace the shattered bones. A metal bar (called a pin) had been inserted through the flesh and bone of my left leg to connect me to a contraption that sat at the foot of my bed and was secured to the floor by several heavy weights. It produced a constant pull that adjusted my leg, so that my hip would reset in its proper position.

My lungs were deteriorating.

Despite my family's prayers and praise, the storm was not letting up, as it had appeared to just after my surgery. Without explanation, my lungs began to fail. The doctors were terribly concerned. "The machine is barely keeping her alive," they said.

Still Mama refused to give up.

One particular morning, when my family arrived to visit, the surgeon asked Mama if he could discuss new measures for my care. He led her down a long hallway to a laboratory, where he showed her the most recent X-rays of my lungs. Mama wept as the surgeon sadly explained that I was no longer breathing on my own. Before Mama could muster up the strength to ask what was next, the surgeon explained that I would need plastic lungs to stay alive. And although the transplant surgery was my only hope, it wasn't an option at this time. I was too sick to endure such an invasive procedure.

Filled with despair, Mama rested her face in her hands and asked God to give her strength. The surgeon continued to show Mama the X-rays. My lungs were deteriorating and becoming more diseased. I had a condition called acute respiratory distress syndrome, which could leave me with debilitating mental, physical, or cognitive issues that would limit my quality of life. He then drew her attention to the white spots on my lungs—the diseased areas. This was why I needed the transplant. The surgeon inhaled deeply and then reluctantly explained that my lungs were disappearing before their eyes and there was nothing they could do to stop it. Finally, he suggested they either pull the plug or transfer me to a hospital that might be better equipped to meet my needs. He couldn't guarantee I'd survive the trip to the next facility, though.

Mama and the surgeon returned to the family to inform them of the two options and explain what a transfer entailed. Due to my critical state and the complex machines connected to my body, it would be impossible to transfer me by ambulance or helicopter. I'd need to be transported to another hospital in a vehicle similar to an eighteen-wheeler. It would be able to transport me and all the equipment that was keeping me alive, but not any of my family.

Mama wept in Carmen's arms and begged the staff to allow her to ride with me. They attempted to comfort Mama as they explained why family members couldn't be inside the truck during the transfer. There was the grave possibility that the rough city roads could jolt the machinery and cause any one of my lifelines to be disconnected, resulting in death. In fact, my chances of surviving the trip were slim, so it would be better if the family met me at the hospital.

Time was of the essence. A decision needed to be made immediately. The surgeons weren't going to allow me much more time at their facility.

Carmen lifted Mama from her arms and suggested they discuss the decision with the family. Mama walked to the waiting room, where several family members sat. Wails of despair filled the room as she and Carmen informed them of the situation. Some of my loved ones, gripped by fear, told Mama to pull the plug, but Mama believed wholeheartedly that it wasn't time. Some wanted the surgeons to give me more time at the current hospital, in hopes that I would improve. But this option was grim as the surgeons had thrown in the towel. Their hospital lacked the technology to help me any further. A decision had to be made. The atmosphere was one of confusion, hostility, and division. Finally, Mama demanded everyone to be silent. She said she wasn't ready to pull the plug and would have me transferred, despite the high risk. Tempers flared, tension was high. Mutual agreement wouldn't be possible. So Mama gathered herself and left the room to pray on her own.

Not long after, Mama returned to the waiting room with tear-filled eyes, a flushed face, and her body bowed slightly. She had decided. She would not allow me to be pulled off the ventilator. I would be transferred.

With great anxiety, everyone gathered their purses, coats, and pillows. They would carpool to the University of Maryland Medical Center (UMMC) Shock Trauma Center in Baltimore, MD. Mama and Carmen returned to my room to hug me one more time. Touching my body with anointing oil, they prayed for every tube to remain intact during the transfer. Then Mama began to remove the cards from the walls. Carmen gathered the CD player and other items around the room. Already informed of Mama's decision, the staff came to say their farewells. One by one the staff hugged Mama and Carmen, hoping to give them strength for what was to come. Tears filled Mama's and Carmen's eyes as they stumbled out the door. Leaving was difficult, but there was nothing more to be said.

Monica M. Johnson

Mama, Carmen, and other family members arrived at UMMC hours before I did. In a designated area they quietly awaited the report of my arrival. No one spoke a word. They all wondered if Mama had made the right decision. A couple of hours later, Mama was told I had arrived but my condition was unknown. The emergency medical staff needed time to get me into a room and confirm that I was stable. Two hours after that, the daunting wait was over: the transfer had been a success. My family joined in prayer, thanking God.

The Shock Trauma Center was well prepared to care for me. Instead of placing me in a standard hospital bed, they securely pinned my body to a flat board. Then, as ordered by the attending physician, the board was rotated temporarily flipping me faced down then back in the supine position in hopes of improving my lung function. Board rotation was a relatively new procedure that couldn't guarantee improvement. In short, it was performed as a desperate attempt to keep me alive.

Day after day, Mama covered my walls with get-well cards. The note about "no negativity" was placed on the door to my room. Mama continued to anoint me from head to toe. She spoke directly to my body, as if my organs and tissues had ears to hear her. Not caring if she appeared foolish, she waited patiently for a miracle. There were some people who questioned Mama's faith. They asked if she felt like giving up, or if she wished that God would allow me to die to free me from the suffering. Mama would respond confidently that a miracle was possible. She'd often go into a quiet space within her mind to remind herself to believe and not doubt.

It had been five long weeks since the tragic accident and since I'd been put on the ventilator. My family had once again set a schedule that allowed visitors to be with me around the clock. The snow continued. January had turned to February and March. Often, a tear would trickle along my face when family talked to me. The family would rejoice, as they believed the tears signaled that I could hear them. The medical staff reminded them that any celebration would be premature at this point. Still no signs of change.

Only Believe

In my semi-comatose state, I began to dream. I wouldn't know that I was sick or where I was. I could hear the machines, but not to the point of consciousness. It was at nighttime, when the lights were dim and the halls were quiet, that I would awaken. I'd try to open my eyes but couldn't, so I was unable to make sense of what was happening around me. The compressions of the ventilator made me think that someone was in the room with me. In that moment, I dreamed that Vanessa was present. There she was, lying on a table next to me. There was a black hose connected to my back, somehow. The sounds were coming from the hose. It echoed sounds of breathing. It gave life. It breathed life back to me. The other end was connected to Vanessa. I couldn't see her, but I felt her presence. I was able to rest and not labor or worry because she was present and breathing for me as I drifted in and out of sleep.

No one seemed to notice my intermittent waking. I started being able to open my eyes occasionally, and in doing so, I felt the stillness of the room. It was peaceful. I would slowly scan the wall. The cards along it spoke volumes. They created a sense of not being alone. Each time I opened my eyes, the greeting cards were clearer. Time was passing, unbeknownst to me. Sometimes I connected to the love and energy in each card. The array of colors, sizes, and creativity provided warmth and comfort.

And then one day, an unseen presence welcomed me back to life. It told me, without words or sound, that the silence was over. Unaware that I had been absent, I was back. I was present again. The fight to remain was over, and the sleep was no more. Then I closed my eyes and instead of darkness, a bright light appeared. It was not a vision of a tunnel leading to a bright light, as others who have died and come back often report. I did not see Heaven or loved ones who had passed on. I saw no faces or figures, nor did I hear a voice. Instead, I saw a brilliant cross. It shone with a light that filled the entire room. It didn't seem strange to me. It didn't yield bewilderment. Instead, it yielded peace and comfort.

Monica M. Johnson

I saw it for a brief moment in time. As quickly as it had appeared it disappeared. But its effects would soon be fully witnessed.

The staff still weren't aware of my consciousness. I don't know if I was asleep or awake on this particular day, but I could hear these words being spoken to me: "Only believe." The voice did not tell me to be courageous. Nor did it instruct me to not be afraid. The voice simply and softly said, "Only believe." I could sense that God was with me and I would be fine, no matter the outcome. I was not alone. I just had to believe that everything was under God's control.

The ventilator was the first sign that something was changing for the better. The medical staff adjusted its dials, as I needed less assistance with my breathing. The family was informed and hoping this would be a progressive change for the better.

Mama stood over my bed and gently touched my forehead, wanting to remove the shattered pieces of glass that remained hidden in my hair. She rested her warm hands on my chest, arms, belly, legs, and feet. Then she asked if I knew where I was and what day it was. Still unable to speak or move my body, I stared into her eyes, expecting her to give me an answer. She gently touched my face and explained that I was in the hospital because I had been in a car accident. Unable to comprehend it all, I drifted back to sleep.

The next time I woke, Mama was gone. As I lay there, I remembered the bright light in the form of a cross. I couldn't recall if it had appeared to me days or only minutes ago. I searched along the walls for "the light." Nothing. I focused and refocused my eyes, hoping to see that light again among the greeting cards. Still nothing. I was almost certain that I had confused the vision with one of the many cards. I scanned them over and over again but couldn't find a single image that resembled the light I'd seen. I became somewhat anxious about the vision and my inability to see it again. Suddenly, in my anxiety, I became aware of the words to a song I'd once heard: "Don't Be Afraid." It's a song about God encouraging Peter (from the Bible) to walk out on the water (to believe). I felt at ease once again and drifted back to sleep.

Monica M. Johnson

7. Point of No Return

I love you, Lord; you are my strength. (Psalm 18:1, NLT)

A Major Milestone

My healing continued, unexpectedly and quickly. In fact, the pace of my healing stunned my many physicians. I had hope, but not without fear. My courage was low. Yet, I was determined to believe that God was with me. I knew that "the light" I'd seen was more than an image in my head. It stuck with me and remained a source of strength for the milestones to come. I can only conclude that it contributed to the amazing miracles I experienced.

My body was thin and frail, but my lungs showed signs of strength and began to function on their own. Soon, I had no need for the ventilator at all. A short time after the ventilator was taken away, a doctor came to my room. He explained that the tube in my left lung had been successfully removed several weeks ago. I couldn't recall this. I'd likely been heavily sedated. They'd also attempted to remove the tube in my right lung, but the lung had collapsed, so they'd had to reinsert the tube. The surgeon explained that there was a possibility it could collapse again.

Unable to respond, I silently listened. Although I was still heavily medicated, I was frightened about the possibility that the lung could collapse again, and about the potential pain. My family wasn't aware that the procedure was about to take place, so no one was at my side. I began to cry and closed my eyes, wishing I weren't alone. I asked God to help me as my anxiety began to get the best of me. I could hear the nurse preparing the area for the doctor. Then, as the doctor was putting on his gloves, my aunt Olivia walked into the room—just in time to hold my hand.

My eyes were still closed. The doctor carefully positioned my arm slightly upward but not above my head. It appeared that my range of motion was limited. Aunt Olivia held my hand tightly. I could hear her praying for me and I knew I was safe. The doctor instructed me to take a deep breath in, and then I felt a sensation of great pressure as the tube was quickly snatched from my side. He immediately pressed on the opening with his other hand. I felt as if I'd had the wind knocked out of me. Would my lung remain expanded? Was I going to continue breathing?

After catching my breath, I realized a miracle had occurred. I wasn't getting a lot of air into my lungs, but I was breathing. I was okay.

I opened my eyes to look at Aunt Olivia. But there was no one there. She had been there, but only in my mind. Another milestone achieved, and I hadn't been alone.

Unimaginable Foretelling

Soon after the tube was removed, another doctor hastily entered the room and told me it was time to remove the pin from my leg—it was time to take me out of the contraption setting my rebuilt pelvis into alignment. I nervously waited for a nurse to numb me, assuming the removal would be painful. But without warning, the doctor swiftly pulled the pin out. I felt nothing. I was thoroughly relieved that yet another procedure had been painless.

Although I was in the process of healing, I had a way to go yet. My legs and my left forearm were paralyzed, and an extra bone had grown in my shoulder, a condition called hyperosteogeny (also known as hypertrophic osteopathy or HO), making it impossible for me to lift my arms above my head. And my atrophic muscles made it impossible for me to be mobile in any sense. I was too weak to sit up on my own, let alone reposition myself in the bed. I would lie there day after day, drifting in and out of sleep.

Monica M. Johnson

But one day, I was awakened by a voice. I opened my eyes to an empty room. The voice said to me, "I want to use you in the deaf community." I was confused—how could I possibly be used in the deaf community, given my limited use of my arms and hands? I drifted off to sleep once more. But the voice woke me again: "I want to use you in the deaf community."

Impossible, I thought. I just didn't have the energy to try to figure out how.

The following day, it was time to remove the trach from my neck—the next major milestone. I was no longer connected to the ventilator, instead I was receiving oxygen through the nasal cannula (tubing). I'd had a peaceful night, with no complications from having the tube removed from my lung.

My lung specialist arrived and stood at the entrance of my room for a few moments before I became aware of his presence. He said nothing, only stared at me as I gasped for air and engaged in small talk with the visitors at my bedside. Speaking was extremely difficult and tiring.

When I noticed the specialist, I stared back at him, waiting for him to speak. Alarmed, I finally broke the silence. I reached for breath and, in my soft, frail voice, asked, "Wha?" What I meant was *Why are you looking at me like that?*

He gulped noticeably, as if there were something stuck in his throat. "You're not supposed to be able to talk!"

I was unaware of the impact a tracheotomy had on speaking, or that a person wasn't supposed to be able to talk while the trach tube is still in the throat. When someone has a trach tube in their neck, air no longer passes over the vocal folds, so the person cannot produce sounds easily. In some cases, the person might be able to make a few sounds but will quickly run out of air. I had somehow pushed air around the trach tube to converse with those around me.

The doctor had come with a valve that would allow me to begin training to speak. But it was clear that I was able to speak *without* this aid! He shook his head in disbelief and kindly dismissed the visitors from my room. Still, seeing that I was able to speak he continued to proceed with adding the valve to what would be an opening in my neck. As a nurse handed him the valve, I lay my head back on the pillow. Then I felt his hand gently pressing against the trach tube. Unable to attach the device that would help me talk, he asked the nurse to hand him a piece of tape. Then, with the strangest look on his face, he said I didn't need the valve. After removing the trach, he placed the tape to the opening that was left. He gave me additional oxygen through a nasal tube and left the room.

At the time, I was unaware of what exactly had transpired, but it was clear that I'd reached another milestone.

Unable to Feel

The next day came with new challenges. On this day of healing, I was faced with a more interesting issue. Now that I was breathing on my own, it was no longer necessary for me to stay in bed. It was time for me to be transferred into a chair for a short period. I couldn't feel my legs, nor did I have the strength to use my arms, and the process of being transferred quickly became emotionally overwhelming. Feeling utterly helpless, I began to cry. The nurse told me not to be alarmed, as the paralysis wasn't permanent, but her words brought me no comfort.

With all of her strength and focus, she lifted me to the edge of the bed. Though she was clearly skilled in what she was doing, I was still terrified she would drop me. I wouldn't be able to catch myself if I slipped out of her grip. Starting to panic, I pleaded with her to not take me any further and to put me back into the bed. My breaths were short, as my lungs couldn't yet take deep breaths or recover quickly from exertion. With the weight of my body pressing heavily against hers, the nurse let me regain my composure as best as I could. In a sitting position, my head hung low and my eyes looking downward, all I could see were these thin, dark, fragile legs before me. They were my legs. I could see them, but I couldn't feel them or move them even slightly. I was completely exhausted, and wanted nothing more than to go back to sleep and wish this moment away.

Her arms firmly around my body, the nurse then gently slid me closer to the edge of the bed. After placing my arms on her shoulders, she embraced me tightly, clasping her hands together around my back. Then she said at the count of three she would lift me into the chair.

Instantly I became dizzy and began to weep again. She allowed me to rest for just a moment more, and then she lifted me off the bed. The chair, which was lined with linen and dressings, was directly next to my bed, so she pivoted cautiously and then carefully placed me into it. I clung to her desperately, wanting her to hold on to me longer. Instead, she rested me against the back of the chair and stepped away. I cried and cried and cried. I couldn't stop crying. Though the threat of falling was over, fear continued to grip me. I was paralyzed by grief. Emotionally, I couldn't get beyond the fact that I was unable to walk and could hardly breathe upon any exertion.

That's when my good friend Stephen walked into the room. He immediately comforted me, reassuring me that I was going to be fine, and I gained control of my breathing and tears.

The chair transfer wasn't a one-time occurrence. It was to become part of my daily therapy in my journey toward complete recovery. Having to sit in the chair each morning was emotionally difficult and physically exhausting. The transfer left me feeling light-headed, dizzy, disoriented, and sad. Each day, I sat for longer periods of time—fifteen minutes then twenty then thirty. And after a couple of weeks the transfer was into a wheelchair.

The Storm of Addiction

My physical strength was improving and the threat of death was gone. Still, isolated storms developed. The cloud of addiction hovered. The doctors decided to not only take me off the IV narcotics (pain medication) but reduce the amount of narcotics that I was receiving. My body wanted and needed the pain meds, so this was my new challenge.

I was still unable to move around on my own, so most of the time I was lying in bed, where I cried daily for the pain medication. I begged and pleaded with the nurses to give me more. They gave me medication in pill form, but I wanted a "quick shot" through my IV. They refused. I felt desperate. I had premonitions of finding a syringe filled with meds. My reasoning was completely distorted. I looked around my room hoping that a syringe filled with morphine had been left inadvertently in my reach. I surely did not want those pain pills. My thought was that if I did find a syringe, I would drop my limp body from the bed onto the cold concrete floor (which I'd once been afraid of falling on) and somehow drag it to where the syringe was.

I was extremely frustrated and angry with everyone. The yearning was painful and grueling. There were no words to comfort me, and it was only the beginning of the weaning process.

I began to hallucinate. I was being taunted mentally. I envisioned cartoon characters in my ceiling, their eyes watching me constantly. Then I envisioned butterflies flying above my bed. I had daydreams and nightmares of all kinds. The storm of addiction was more like a war. It was as if the drug itself were calling me by name—it had a gruesome invitation to freely indulge, but I couldn't get to it. I yearned to get out of bed and respond to the meds' call. I wanted them as much as they seemed to want me. As the war waged in my mind, I felt like I wanted to die.

Monica M. Johnson

During each day of the weaning process, the doctors explained to Mama that I was being weaned and what to expect from my behavior as a result of the weaning process. As she sat at my bedside, Mama longed to help me. She constantly reassured me that there were no eyes watching me and that she couldn't get me IV medication. She prayed for the bout of addiction to pass quickly. Visit after visit, Mama watched my body shake, as my thoughts and fears got the best of me, until suddenly…

It was over. Just like that, I was free from the addiction.

God's "Angels"

Unlike the critically ill and unconscious patients in the shock trauma unit, I was awake and able to articulate my pains and fears. And I was making way too much noise to remain on this floor. My constant crying and complaining signaled to the staff that my condition had improved. I longed to leave the hospital and return home with Mama. However, the doctors told Mama that I had a long road to recovery—discharge would not be my next step.

It was too soon for me to go to a rehabilitation center, so my next move was to another floor in the hospital, a step below shock trauma. I still needed to be constantly observed and cared for. My mind was foggy. I didn't want to be switched to another floor.

On the day I was to be transferred, the surgeons found a questionable spot on one of my lungs. They informed me that until they could properly diagnose my condition, I would have to remain where I was. The surgeons were perplexed, as they'd been monitoring my lungs constantly.

Each day I remained in the shock trauma unit, I grew more lonely at night, after Mama and the rest of the family went home. The loneliness brought fears of sleeping, and I began dreading nighttime. It seemed the family's prayers did not go unanswered, as one day, I received two nighttime "angels": Ed, who was an orderly, and Sherry, who was an X-ray technician. Both were Christians.

At night, the hallway lights were turned off, as well as the lights in the patients' rooms, and the nurses' station light was dimmed. There were no sounds aside from those of the monitors throughout the unit. On separate occasions, Ed and Sherry would stroll through the hallway. As I softly wept in the dark, they would be drawn into my room. They would quietly approach my bed and gently lift my hand, placing it in their own. The warmth of their presence and the touch of their hands made me feel safe.

I can recall one particular occasion when Ed entered my room. His voice was low, his expression neutral. He always spoke softly and slowly. As I cried, he asked, "Sis, why are you crying? God has not forgotten about you." Then, as he often did, he prayed with me until the morning, when I finally fell asleep. Then there was Sherry—Sherry who was always smiling and wearing an expression that said, "Everything is all right, there's no need for worrying." On occasion she'd pull up a chair next to my bed and hold my hand as she talked about the love of God. And she would stay until my tears had ceased and my mind was at ease.

The morning proved to surround me with angels as well. It seemed that whenever I was struggling the most I was sent a nurse name Sharon. Sharon had a big heart and made everything light and "okay" with her warm sense of humor. She cared for me as if I were her longtime friend. Many times, she'd visit me to see that my needs were met even if she hadn't been assigned to me for the day. Sharon made me happy, especially when she joked with me. Sometimes she'd perfectly mimic my whining and crying to leave. Before she left my side, I would tell her that I loved her. She'd reply sincerely but in a voice that reminded me of the frog on the Budweiser commercial: "I love you too, man."

I was also blessed with a nurse named Nancy, a tall redhead who'd graduated high school with Vanessa and Malissa. Often she'd check up on me and reassure my family that she'd be there for me.

Monica M. Johnson

Despite my "angels," I still cried all the time—usually because I wanted to leave the hospital with the last person who'd visited me for the day. Sadness would immediately fill my heart whenever a visitor had to leave. According to the physicians, I wouldn't be leaving any time soon. The plan of action for my recovery would have me remain at the UMMC for a year and then transfer to a rehabilitation hospital for another year. And then home. It seemed I would be crying for a long time.

My New Home

The emergency medical technician (EMT) arrived in my room with Mama and a gurney. I was to be transported to the Montebello Rehabilitation Center (currently Kernan Rehabilitation Center) in Baltimore, MD, by ambulance. Among the physicians, an agreement had been reached: I was ready for the rehabilitation center, six months earlier than originally predicted. Somehow I was ready for the change.

The ride to my new "home" was almost like a leisure ride. The sirens weren't piercing the air, nor did we travel at a high speed. I casually talked about the accident with the EMT and completed the pertinent forms. The transfer happened so quickly I had no time to process what was to come. The rehab center was just a few miles from the UMMC.

The center would be my new home for the year, according to the doctors. When we arrived and I saw the outside of this new home, oddly enough I cried and begged Mama not to make me stay there. The building was old and ugly. It triggered me to feel afraid. Without a word, she wiped the tears that rolled along my face and kept her hands close to my body to quiet my mind.

Once I was in my room, my tears gave way to fear. I was sharing a room with quadriplegics. Why had I been placed with quadriplegics? Had my situation changed? Was I not going to receive feeling in my legs again? Had my story changed? Had the doctors been keeping silent until now?

I watched Mama, who always showed kindness to strangers. She was chatting with a patient who sat in a wheelchair, and I heard the woman tell Mama that she'd been in a car accident. I began to cry once more. Mama came to me and rubbed my face. Just before the EMT was about to transfer me into my bed, they got a call: there had been a mix-up. Much to my relief, the front desk had given them the wrong floor.

As the EMT rolled me through the well-lit hallway, I wondered how I would endure my time here. It was gloomy. The building smelled old and made me feel sad. In my room were four beds. Mine was closest to the door, which I liked. It made me feel as though I wasn't boxed in. A sturdy steel arm extended from the wall at the head of the bed and connected to a small outdated television. An elderly woman was in the bed directly across from mine, and a young woman named Kisha was in the bed to my right. The bed across from Kisha's was empty. To my surprise, Kisha was destined to become my friend. We had a few things in common. We both loved the Lord. We'd both been in car accidents. We'd both been transferred from shock trauma. And we were both "crybabies."

Kisha and I cried about everything. We cried because our bath water was cold. We cried because the nurses didn't answer our calls immediately. We cried when we got our heparin shots (blood thinners). We cried when family left. We cried because we couldn't get comfortable at night. Sometimes we cried when we didn't have anything else to do. I wondered if our brains had no control over our crying anymore as a result of our accidents. Most of the time it felt as if I had no control of my emotions. But now, I had Kisha—we had each other. Kisha and I encouraged each other and prayed aloud for each other, sharing our tears and our belief to live "normal" again.

My family personalized my new room with encouraging posters, greeting cards from friends and family, and the CD player. As the days went by, I began accepting my new home a little more.

Monica M. Johnson

On one particular day, my family stayed with me the entire day. Before leaving for the evening, they helped me to get as comfortable as possible in the bed and then prayed with me. I slept fine through the night. The next morning I felt refreshed, stronger, and confident. Well, that is, until I was given my own wheelchair! It was placed next to my bed, and the nurse gestured it was for me. This time I was unable to process what the chair meant in this stage of my recovery. The chair seemed to scream setback, and sent me into a panic.

I cried and cried. In fact, I cried so much that my blood pressure became alarmingly elevated. Even Kisha was unable to calm me. The medical staff warned me that if I didn't calm down, I'd be taken back to shock trauma. I told them that I'd stop crying, but I couldn't. I had difficulty breathing, and my vitals became unstable. The staff called my house repeatedly, hoping to get Mama. No one answered. The ambulance was called, and I was rushed to the emergency room at the UMMC, where the doctors began to examine me immediately. An IV was inserted in my arm. Sometime between my arrival in the ER and the transfer to the hospital bed, I had stopped crying. Soon, I was rolled into a special lab for several lung tests.

I was terrified that something major was going wrong. Having no one to hold my hand, I began to pray. A technician conducting a test communicated with me from outside the room, through an intercom. I held my breath when the technician prompted me to. The test showed there was no damage to my lungs, and I was soon released to return to the rehab center.

That night, I was no longer worried about the wheelchair, and sleep came easily. Waking the next morning, I was hopeful that I wouldn't relapse. Everything inside me felt weak, but I was certain it was time to be strong and trust God. I accepted the wheelchair as a tool to help me walk again.

My real test was patience. I had to learn how to be patient and allow others to help me. I was still catheterized because my bladder was leaking fluid internally. I spoke with an impediment, as if I'd had a stroke. My vision wasn't clear; everything appeared blurred, like a movie being played on fast-forward times ten. I couldn't get in or out of the bed without supervision; I was unable to walk or feel my left leg. When I wasn't encouraging Kisha to be patient, she was surely encouraging me to be.

As early as five in the morning, Kisha and I would have our lukewarm or cold "birdbaths." The "birdbath" was a small basin set up on our bedside table to wash our body best as we could verses having a shower. Kisha and I often cried because we didn't have hot water or anyone who cared that our water was never hot. It was difficult for me to bathe myself because I had partial feelings in my left hand and limited mobility in my right hand, couldn't lift my arms, had very little upper body strength, and was easily exhausted. I was also unable to dress myself, which made my morning a daunting task that required persistence and willpower. It seemed most of the staff were not very friendly, empathetic, or helpful.

After our "birdbaths," we had to wait for the physicians to make their rounds. I had several open wounds on my left leg (from the removal of the pins), which needed new dressings each morning. All this before we received breakfast. Patience was the key!

My days consisted of occupational therapy, physical therapy, visits with doctors concerning my ailments, and rest. Occupational therapy, which took place down the hallway from my room, involved working on my sensory motor skills and cognitive skills. It also taught me coordination, so that I'd be able to use my hands again. The doctors had been unable to diagnose the cause of the numbness and partial paralysis in my left hand and forearm. The therapist often had me play with cold, uncooked rice in a bag to desensitize the area that hurt when touched. The paralysis was in the pinky and ring fingers and along the forearm. The doctor said that if therapy didn't help, invasive surgery to cut out tissue and reconstruct the nerves might be required. But for now, I would endure the intense therapy each day.

Occupational therapy also taught me basic self-care, including bathing, dressing, and feeding myself. The tasks were difficult to complete. Often I'd become exhausted and end up in tears because I thought the nurses were asking too much of me. They would tell me to keep trying and reassure me that I could do it. Slowly but surely, I made progress. The first time I completely dressed myself without assistance, I cried—but this time it was for joy.

Physical therapy involved strengthening and conditioning my muscles. Like occupational therapy, it was intense, but in a different way. The sessions took place outside of my bedroom, in a room that had several low, long tables, weights, beds, and training equipment. Walkers, wheelchairs, and crutches were also available along the walls. Physical therapy taught me how to transfer myself from the bed to the wheelchair so that I'd eventually be able to get in and out of the bed without supervision. I was given various exercises with light weights to strengthen my body as a whole.

Along my belly were over seventy staples, which had keloids. (A keloid is a thick, elevated, irregularly shaped scar.) These scars needed special attention. It was not a requirement of the physical therapist, yet often she would massage them and attempted to teach me how to flatten the raised areas. Unable to touch or even look at the scars, I was unsuccessful with treating the keloids myself.

Going Home

My rehab stay was shockingly short. In one month's time, I had strengthened my body enough to maneuver in and out of the bed on my own. I had gained the full use of my right hand and enough use of my left hand to feed and dress myself. And what was most astonishing was the fact that I had regained feeling in my legs—I was mobile once again. I mainly used the wheelchair but was able to move slowly with crutches or a walker.

I was still restricted when it came to bearing weight on my left side, where my pelvis was shattered, and could only lie in bed in certain positions. And the dark cloud concerning my bladder lingered. Instead of being released to return home, I was transferred by ambulance to UMMC for additional surgery. The physicians had learned that there were bone fragments from my shattered pelvis imbedded in my bladder. These bone fragments were to be removed, in hopes that my bladder would heal. If the surgery was successful, I would be able to remove the catheter. My family packed my belongings once I left, but I exchanged contact information with Kisha prior to our separating. I looked forward to spending time with her in the future—she had been a great support during my time at the rehab center.

The time with Kisha had strengthened my faith. Surprisingly, I felt little anxiety on my way to surgery. Mama and Daddy met me at the hospital. They both held my hands and prayed for me as I lay waiting to be taken into the operating room. I was more concerned about the condition of my lungs. I hoped they were strong enough to be put under general anesthesia. The anesthesiologist comforted me, saying they knew about my lungs and were prepared to handle any emergency situation. She reminded me that she would remain with me the entire time and that I was strong enough for the surgery.

Monica M. Johnson

Upon putting me to sleep for the surgery, the surgeon soon discovered scar tissue, which would prevent intubation (the placement of a flexible plastic tube in my trachea to maintain an open airway during surgery). An alternative method was successfully administered, and surgery was on as scheduled. There were no complications, and within a couple of hours the surgery was complete.

Mama and Daddy accompanied me from the recovery room to the hospital room, where I was to remain under observation for a few days. Assuming my recovery would be easy, they left for the night with no reservations. But the morphine drip seemed to only put me to sleep, as I'd feel intense pain upon waking. And this time I had no "angels" that I could see, and the staff wasn't very pleasant. I was in pain and I felt alone. I prayed constantly.

Luckily, two days after the surgery, my release papers were signed, instructions were given, and Mama was ready to take me home. Though I was looking forward to going home, the surgery had zapped the strength I'd gained from rehab, and I felt I'd been set back ten steps from the twelve that I'd gained. The fall I took while climbing the steps into the house proved my digression.

As I attempted to use the crutches to maneuver up the steps, I lost my footing and slipped backward into the arms of my brother. No one had wanted to carry me and risk misaligning the pelvic plates. Tears fell along my face as my brother took away the crutch. Without another thought, he lifted me up and carried me into the house.

Exhausted, I wanted nothing more than to go to bed. Mama and Junior got me settled quickly. Nobody knew what to expect at this point. Nobody knew the chain of events to come.

Only a few hours after I was discharged, my body began to yearn for pain medication. My emotions were unbalanced—I was angry, aggressive, and out of control. I was in a rage. Mama had no idea how to help me. She often found herself holding me in her arms and rocking me back and forth. She rubbed my back,

prayed, and sang over me as my body shook. As the days went by, I became weaker, had no appetite, and was fatigued, achy, and irate. It was clear that I was experiencing withdrawal from the narcotics or steroid medications.

Distraught about my condition, Mama phoned the hospital for help. After the staff investigated the situation, they informed Mama that I hadn't been sent home with all the proper medications. Without further delay, the prescriptions were phoned in to a nearby pharmacy.

Another storm passed.

Monica M. Johnson

8. The Apple of His Eye

Keep me as the apple of your eye. (Psalms 17:8, NIV)

A Season of Regression

Though I was finally home, each day was filled with challenges. Before my discharge from the rehabilitation center, I had gained some independence. I was able to get in and out of the bed with no supervision or assistance. I was able to eat solid foods and feed myself. I was able to bathe and dress myself. I was able to use the crutches. Now, suddenly, I wasn't strong enough to do these simple tasks I'd conquered a short time ago.

I also struggled to remember things that had happened prior to the accident, as well as things about myself—likes and dislikes, etc. The faces of the people who visited me were familiar, but I couldn't figure out what kind of emotional bond we shared. I felt so lost and out of place. The story of my car accident and the pain that everyone endured totally overwhelmed me. I thought my heart would explode from sadness as I listened to my family tell me how afraid they were of losing me, and of the pain they felt seeing me suffer. It seemed as if the story wasn't even about me. I couldn't look at the photos of the demolished car or listen to the tape recording of my son, nieces, and nephews praying for me. It was too much to endure.

In addition to the mental anguish, I felt pain in every part of my body. With every tiring breath I felt my fractured ribs. The pain in my pelvic area radiated through my bones, muscles, and tendons with every move I made. I was so thin and fragile I could feel either pins or bones when I sat on a hard surface. The pain in my neck spread down my back. I felt tired and fatigued all the time. It was difficult to get comfortable. My head ached, my heart throbbed, and my mind was filled with questions about my future. I was riddled with fear of the unknown.

Friends told me to "get into the Word," but I had no clue what that really meant. Some said God had a plan for my life and He was going to use me. But my mind was in a fog. I found myself unable to comprehend the things of God. I was being challenged to remain faithful to a God I couldn't see. My heart was burdened with grief.

The mental fog not only challenged my faith but also my emotional connection with Walter, my son. As I regarded my nine-year-old, I felt no maternal connection. The son with whom I had spent every day laughing, loving, and living had become a little boy with whom I couldn't connect. I looked at him as if I didn't know him. In his eyes was an expression of worry and sincere concern. He clearly needed and expected something from me, but I couldn't remember "us"—who we were together. He'd hug me ever so gently. He'd cautiously watch my every move. His eyes questioned if I would live or die. And yet, at twenty-seven years old, I lay in bed like a little girl yearning for my mama.

I couldn't sleep unless Mama lay in the bed with me. I was afraid to fall asleep if Mama wasn't holding me tightly, protecting me from the fears that resided deep within my thoughts and dreams. She'd hold me snugly, and I'd feel her warm breath and rhythmic heartbeat against my frail body. I'd mimic her breaths and my heart would mimic the rhythm of her heart and I would know I was okay. I was alive.

Monica M. Johnson

The nights Mama had to work, Carmen and Junior cared for me. Carmen would lie next to me, just as Mama did. She held me and loved me as if I were her baby. She seemed sad, and was quiet. I sensed her longing to make everything all right as she read Bible stories to me night after night. Still I cried. When I cried, she would sit closer to me, the Bible open in her lap, and sing. She sang about God's love for me and how much Jesus loved me. I'm certain she sang for hours, sometimes until the sun was rising. "Yes, Jesus loves you…"

Junior never held me physically, but he was always close by. His love and deep concern held me, just as the arms of Mama and Carmen did. I doubt that he ever slept peacefully. At this point, I was barely able to lift my head. Every night he spent half an hour to an hour trying to get me comfortable in the bed, positioning and repositioning my pillows. The positions I could lie in were limited due to the tension and tightness in my neck, shoulders, and head. And because of the pelvic fracture, I couldn't put full pressure on the left side of my body. Some nights Junior came in and out of my room to adjust the pillows so I could sleep. On my bed were pillows of every shape, size, and thickness. There were half-rolled pillows to support my back, pillows tucked between my knees and under my head, and oval pillows beneath my neck and below my belly. I'd reassure him that I was comfortable, but minutes later I'd draw him back to adjust the pillows all over again. He never showed any sign of frustration, though I imagine my beckoning for his help as soon as he sat down in the next room was exhausting for him. No one was able to soothe me as quickly and as easily as Mama. If the pillows weren't the cause of my tears, yearning for Mama was.

Mornings meant Mama was coming home. I waited anxiously to hear the front door open and Mama's footsteps proceeding down the hallway. I weighed less than one hundred pounds (forty pounds less than I'd weighed before the accident). And each morning, without fear of reinjuring me, Mama would gently lift my body into a sitting position to hug me. I trusted Mama completely. I was never afraid she would drop me.

Immediately upon her return, Mama was at work to get me all better. Before walking into my bedroom, she'd adjust the heat in the bathroom, making the temperature perfect for my morning wash. The bathroom adjacent to my bedroom was set up for my morning ritual. In the bathroom was a rented portable toilet. Mama would put the lid down and cushion it with a thick pillow. She'd also place several towels around the metal support bars for comfort. A small basin of hot water mixed with several drops of olive oil and baby wash was placed on a towel in front of the toilet. Next to the basin were bottles of olive oil, baby lotion, and baby powder, a washcloth, and a towel. After wheeling me to the entrance of the bathroom, Mama would lift my weak body out of the wheelchair and carefully place me on the pillow. I'd hold on to the safety bars, attempting to assist her. Once I was secure on the seat, she would push the wheelchair into the hallway and close the door to keep the room heated. Then, Mama thoroughly bathed me, from my head to my toes. She'd humbly kneel before me to wash my feet. My emotional connection to Mama remained strong—she was the only person I was able to connect with sometimes. I was filled with gratitude and love for her. I appreciated and adored her so much that I often felt sad to see her working so hard to rehabilitate me.

After bathing me, Mama would empty the contents of my catheter bag. She'd tenderly massage my body with lotion and anointing oil and pamper me with a powder rub as well. As she clothed me, she'd wipe my tears repeatedly, reassuring me that she loved me. Although Mama did all the work, after this ritual, I would be completely exhausted and need to rest. Mama would carry me back into the bedroom and gently put me in bed. Then she'd let me nap while she prepared my breakfast, which would sometimes become brunch, depending on how long I slept.

Monica M. Johnson

I was fed every two hours. Although I'd been eating solid food at the rehabilitation center, now I could tolerate only liquids. I was both frustrated and confused about my relapse. It was as if I had never been through rehabilitation at all. Mama began to teach me to feed, bathe, and dress myself, and constantly reassured me that I would one day be stronger and independent. She encouraged me to be patient.

A Season of Restoration

Mama was correct. As time went on, I began overcoming my limitations. The paralyzed hand no longer deterred me. I started attempting to wash myself. Mama still heated the bathroom for me, prepared the basin of water, and placed everything I needed within reach. I was determined to complete the ritual alone, but many times I fell short. Mama would return to the bathroom only to find me sitting on the cushioned toilet out of breath and crying. I would reluctantly surrender to her help and return to the bedroom to rest and regain my composure, holding on to hope for a better day.

My digestive system had become stronger, so the new challenge was finding foods that I actually liked. My taste buds seemed "off" as I relearned who I was. I had no idea what I'd be able to tolerate from day to day. Nevertheless, I was getting more independent.

Eventually I became strong enough to begin outpatient therapy at the nearby hospital. Three times weekly Mama drove me to the hospital and walked me to the therapy floor. My goals were to increase the range of motion in my shoulders and neck, to regain flexibility throughout my entire body, to gain sensation in my left arm, which was locked slightly above a ninety-degree angle, and to strengthen my core. Basically, I needed total healing for my body, as well as for my mind and spirit. Before leaving the house for therapy, I would rub my left arm and hand with the anointing oil that Mama kept in my bedroom. And each morning I'd close my eyes and say prayers from a little orange book by Walter A. Straughan called *By Jesus' 39 Stripes We Were Healed*. I often took the book to therapy to read during the times I was discouraged by my lack of progress, or when stretching caused intense pain. The meditation on God's Word gave me strength.

After several sessions, I hit a plateau in terms of my left arm's range of motion. The therapist conducted tests that confirmed the need for surgery to remove the extra bone from my shoulders. There was a list of surgeries I'd need once I became stronger, and this one was at the top of the list. The surgeon also suggested having the scar tissue removed from my throat. A band of tissue had fused my vocal cords together, restricting airflow. And finally, I'd need surgery to reconstruct the nerves in my elbow—this would hopefully restore sensation in my left hand and release the elbow's limitation.

With the help of my little orange book, I prayed for a miracle: to be completely physically healed and emotionally whole. Daily, I made it a practice to anoint the troubled areas of my body with oil and to remove negative thoughts from my mind. I wanted every promise that the scriptures spoke of concerning being whole and healed. I read the scriptures every day to keep my mind sharp and clear as physical and mental challenges continued to present themselves.

At the beginning and end of each therapy session, the therapist measured the range of motion of my arms. I would stand with my face toward the wall, the tips of my shoes touching it. While leaning forward, I'd lift one arm at a time. Taking a deep breath in, I'd stretch upward as much as possible while holding my position. As I struggled to lift my arm above my head, the therapist encouraged me to stretch even further, pulling my arm upward. Then, holding my arm firmly against the wall, he'd draw a small line on the wall just above my middle finger. Sometimes the mark would be lower than the previous day's mark. Nevertheless, the mark was made and my goal was set. The measuring was a form of therapy on its own. It stretched me beyond my comfort zone.

Monica M. Johnson

After taking the measurement, the therapist would then perform a deep-tissue massage around my shoulders and arm to relieve the pain. Then he would slowly lift my arm (one arm at a time) above my head, attempting to gain more motion and greater range. On one particular day, something unexpected happened. As he lifted my right arm, the most astounding sound permeated the room. It sounded as if a wooden stick had been broken in two. POP! The extra bone in my shoulder had cracked, separating it from the original bone and releasing the tension in my shoulders. I immediately had full range of motion—but not without pain. The experience momentarily took my breath away. I gasped for air. Silently, I lay there staring at the ceiling as my heart raced. Had the break been a good thing, or was it bad? I didn't know because the therapist was wide-eyed, staring at me.

"Are you okay?" he asked softly. I slowly nodded. He reached over to lift the other arm. Before I could demand he not touch it, he raised it above my head. Again, a pop sounded throughout the room. Once more, the therapist asked if I was okay. And sure enough, I was fine. The snap had caused some pain and anxiety, but it was clear that yes, I was more than okay. I was being healed—without a surgeon.

Within a week of my shoulders' unexpected healing, I saw my surgeons concerning the paralysis in my left arm/hand and the condition of my lungs. I was anxious and downcast about the thought of more surgeries. Here I was once again in the exam room. I was told that the surgery to my arm would be quite invasive, as it would involve making an incision that extended from my elbow to my wrist. The surgeon believed extra tissue and muscle needed to be removed from the elbow and forearm— tissue trapped at the elbow was causing my forearm to lock at a 135-degree angle. Then he would reconstruct the nerves in an attempt to restore feeling. Unfortunately, he couldn't promise that I'd have full use of my arm and hand again, nor could he be certain that I'd no longer experience the paralysis.

The doctor left the room so that Mama and I could discuss everything. As Mama embraced me, I lay my head on her shoulder and cried. I didn't want another surgery, but I wanted full use of my hand. My mind drifted back to something I'd experienced after the bladder surgery, several weeks prior. I recalled vividly a sensation in my belly that made me feel as though I was finished with the surgeries. I was sure I wouldn't have to go back into surgery. Now, given the doctor's new findings, I was confused. I didn't know whether to "trust my gut" or go with the surgeon's professional opinion. Weary, and afraid of making the wrong decision, I walked out of the office with Mama, leaving the status of the surgery pending.

In the same building, minutes later, I visited the lung specialist. My thoughts were consumed with the last appointment, so I had no expectations concerning how this one would play out. The lung specialist had won my trust early on. He had a way of making Mama and me feel comfortable and confident in his abilities. His warm greeting and genuine look of surprise each time he saw me (alive) reminded me of what a miracle I had become and how fortunate I was to be alive. Today's greeting was no different. As he scurried into the room, it was clear that he'd hurried to get to my appointment.

As soon as he popped open the door, he asked how I was feeling and immediately examined the scar on my throat. Today's appointment was about testing the condition of my lungs. However, as mentioned, I'd developed scar tissue on my vocal cords from the tracheostomy. And this scarring could affect the results of the lung testing. I was supposed to have had surgery on my vocal cords prior to the appointment—I was hoping to take the test in spite of the fact that I hadn't.

But I was to be disappointed. According to the doctor, the vocal cord surgery was a must. The scar on my throat was thick and doubled over. Without waiting to hear my explanation as to why I hadn't had the surgery, he explained that I had to have it to get an accurate reading on the condition of my lungs.

Monica M. Johnson

And so, without further ado, he ordered me to have the surgery and made it clear that he wouldn't see me until I'd done so. As he prepared to leave, he told me that he was on his way to attend to a young girl in shock trauma who had been in a car accident and needed a lung transplant—she needed plastic lungs. He looked into my eyes and said, "You were supposed to have the same surgery as this young girl. But we didn't expect you to live, nor were you strong enough for this surgery, so we didn't perform it." He beamed in admiration and hastily shuffled out of the room.

I sat stunned by his words. For a moment, I thought about the little girl and felt empathy. Then I thought about how blessed I was to be breathing without plastic lungs or an oxygen tank. I tried to imagine what my life might have been like, and then my thoughts quickly drifted back to my present situation. How was I going to see the lung specialist again when I believed in my heart that I wasn't supposed to have more surgery? Although I got short of breath whenever I exerted myself, I always recovered quickly. I was certain that my lungs were returning to normal through divine healing, but the doctor's request made it difficult for me to stand on God's Word.

Back at home, I called a few friends who believed in the power of prayer and asked them to pray for me. I believed that God wanted to miraculously heal me. I explained to them that I believed the bladder surgery was supposed to have been my last. When I talked to my pastor, he said that scar-tissue surgery wasn't a big deal and that I should have it and get it out of the way. Another person accused me of being ridiculous and foolish in my faith. No one agreed that I should go without the surgery. I was keenly aware that since the accident, God had healed me in various ways—surgery, blood transfusions, prayer, the laying on of hands, and even the life-support machine. But it wasn't clear to me how God was going to heal me this go around (i.e., through surgery or some other, miraculous, way).

And so, instead of standing on His promise, I went ahead and scheduled the surgery. I had somewhat convinced myself that I was being foolish and needed to walk in wisdom. The night before the surgery, feeling very confused about my decision, I phoned my friend Stephen, a man of great faith. I told him what I believed I'd heard from God. Then he said something that changed my life: "If there's sunshine on every side of the house and the Lord says it's gonna rain, get your umbrella. It's gonna rain!" In other words, no matter what the circumstances or what others might say, if the Lord speaks a word, believe it.

Immediately, the uneasiness left the pit of my belly. Stephen's words made everything clear. The confusion was gone.

The doctor's office was closed, so I couldn't cancel my appointment yet. As I lay in bed falling asleep, I had no idea how God was going to work this miracle, but I was certain He would instruct me. I was waiting for, well, a nudging or a sensing of some sort. I went to bed expecting something great to happen.

The next morning, I woke expecting to experience some sort of divine intervention. Still nothing. Had I missed his instructions? I didn't know, so I remained quiet as I prepared to leave for the hospital. I hadn't said a word to Mama about my expectation of a miracle, so she too prepared herself for the appointment as planned. Without breakfast, water, or dialogue Mama and I left for the hospital. I felt uneasy about going but didn't speak up to tell Mama to cancel my appointment. If God didn't want me to have the surgery, why hadn't I been urged not to go, or somehow detained? I pondered the question as we drove toward the hospital, which was about forty minutes from home.

When we arrived, I was taken to a room with two vacant beds and given a hospital gown. The nurse instructed me not to eat anything and told me the surgeon would be in shortly to talk to me. It was early morning, so I assumed I was one of the first patients on the schedule. I lay in the bed and Mama sat next to it. Daddy arrived shortly to pray over the equipment, the medical staff, and me. Then we all sat quietly, waiting.

Monica M. Johnson

A couple of hours passed with no word. Mama left the room to ask the nurses what was happening. She was told that the surgeon was running behind schedule and I would be the next patient to be wheeled into the operating room. I began to feel hungry, tired, and frustrated, and Daddy began to feel uncomfortable about the wait. He didn't like any form of confusion, as he felt God wasn't present in confusion. So, he excused himself from the room. I'm not sure where he went or what he was sensing, but he was known to pray alone in times such as this. Mama continued to wait with me.

Two more hours passed. This time, I buzzed for the nurse and inquired about the delay. They told me that there had been a mix-up with the schedule and that they would be with me very soon. I began to feel uneasy in the pit of my belly. Still questioning the surgery, I closed my eyes and prayed.

I asked God for peace, for order in the confusion, and for instructions on what I was to do. Then I fell asleep. I have no idea how long I was out, but suddenly I rose straight up in a sitting position. I called for Mama, who had drifted off to sleep as well. I asked her to hand me my clothes, and she frowned in confusion.

While I was asleep, "I heard the Lord say that His hand was not in this surgery," I told her. "It's not time for me to have this surgery. I need to leave." There was too much confusion, and God is not the author of confusion.

As I was getting out of the hospital gown, the nurse entered the room. She wasn't happy when I told her that I was going home. She told me to wait while she contacted the surgeon. When I spoke with him (I'd met him on only one other occasion), he told me that it was important that I have the surgery.

"I understand the repercussions," I said. "But I'm going home."

Agitated, he reluctantly led us to the desk to sign the release forms. The anxiety I'd been feeling was released. How I would get in to see my lung specialist, I had no clue. For now, I was at peace.

Another Bout with Addiction

After I returned home, my lungs took a back seat in my healing process. The paralysis of my arm was at the forefront of my mind. I continued to anoint my left forearm and hand daily. I professed aloud that my left hand would be fully healed. I envisioned using it as I had before the accident.

A few weeks had passed since the miracle of being able to lift my arms when I began experiencing pain in the pinky and ring fingers of my left hand. The pain began suddenly, and it became more intense with each passing day. It originated within the pinky finger and traveled down the outside of my hand. Within days, the intense pain had extended into my palm and up my forearm. Day after day, I cried in agony. I prayed fervently, asking God for relief, but my prayers seemed to go unanswered. I had gone from feeling nothing in this part of my body to feeling excruciating pain.

I began taking more pain meds without doctor's orders. But the pain wouldn't go away, and the meds were gone before it was time for a refill. I was desperate. Desperate to feel better. I called my other doctors to get additional narcotics prescriptions. If my lung specialist didn't prescribe me more pain meds, my bone doctor or bladder doctor or primary care doctor did. Then my primary care doctor became suspicious. I couldn't remember whom I'd called last, and it seemed he'd filled my prescription one too many times. The next time I visited him, he strongly suggested I was addicted to the pain meds and refused to prescribe me more.

Throughout each day, I found myself tapping my wristwatch trying to make the time go by faster so that I could take more pain meds. I was determined to prove the doctor wrong. I was certain I was taking only what I'd been prescribed and only what I needed. But I was in denial. I was addicted.

The family physician gave Mama a printout of all of the narcotics I'd been prescribed in a month's time. Mama convinced me to look at it. It was there in black and white: I was abusing the pain medication. And once again, I needed intervention immediately. Mama controlled the doses of my pain meds from that point on. I was in agony trying to endure the pain from one dose to the next. I would rock back and forth as I sat on the cushioned dining room chair at home to self-soothe. My days were long and the nights were longer. The rocking in the chair turned to fits of rage. I couldn't talk to Mama without getting angry or violent. Once I felt anger, then the rage transformed; I'd cry and ask Mama to hold me as I rocked in the chair. I'd ask her repeatedly why God wouldn't take away this yearning. After all, I believed in His power to do it, so why the delay? Mama said she didn't know why, but she was sure that peace would come and that God was with me.

No matter how much I begged for the pills, Mama stayed strong and wouldn't give in. Slowly, the urge left my body. The weeks of decreasing the meds proved to be beneficial. I returned to normal. The pain in my arm remained, but the yearning for narcotics was gone.

My Pain Was My Blessing

I tried not to lose hope about the condition of my arm. Often, my heart seemed to race with the intensity of the pain that radiated from my fingers. I had been dealing with the pain for weeks now.

And then one day, I became aware of something: the once-paralyzed hand was experiencing sensation. Yes, the sensation was pain, but it was a sensation nonetheless. I realized the pain meant that there were nerves responding to something, or regenerating themselves to the point where I felt the stimulation. Ultimately, my pain was my blessing. I cried with great expectation. Each day, the pain became less intense, and a couple of weeks later, I gained full use of my once-paralyzed hand. I was completely shocked. I felt God had granted me yet another miracle.

With the focus off my hand, it was time to visit the lung specialist again. I have no idea how, but I'd been scheduled for testing without proof of the surgery. At the hospital, I performed a series of breathing tests, which consisted of breathing deeply into several different kinds of plastic tubes while a graph recorded the results on a chart. The results were then printed out on a sheet of paper, which I had to carry to the lung specialist's office the same day. I nervously walked down the hall to his office.

When the lung specialist entered the examining room, he immediately said, "So you had the surgery." I was afraid to answer him—or maybe I was reluctant to answer him so quickly with a lie—so I said nothing. I stared at Mama, expecting her to give me the words to say. She explained to him that I hadn't had the surgery. He stepped closer to me. "Oh. It looks like you've had reconstructive surgery."

I smiled as Mama explained our faith and belief regarding the situation. Then he carefully looked over the test results and explained that although I hadn't soared on the testing, my results were very close to normal. Some of the results were equivalent to that of a person my age with healthy lungs, and others were slightly below the average range. He told me that I was fortunate because the mortality rate for acute respiratory distress syndrome exceeded 40 percent.

"You're my million-dollar patient," he said, and explained that he was totally amazed by my progress. Having received the specialist's blessing, I felt I was ready to function on my own.

Free at last!

Crossing Over

One report after another proved I was becoming physically stronger. But I was still experiencing a lot of fear. When I was in shock trauma, I vowed I would never drive a car again. I was also afraid of traveling over bridges. But one day, without the consent

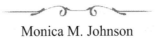

of my outpatient physical therapist, I decided it was time to conquer my fear of driving. And not just that. I would conquer the fear of driving over the very bridge I'd nearly died on. To get to the therapy sessions each week, I had to cross this bridge. Up to this point, Mama had driven me. It had been just five months since the accident, but it seemed like years.

The sky was clear and the sun was shining. I asked Carmen if I could drive her car, and she asked if I'd been cleared to drive alone. I lied, and she handed me the keys. Nervous, I prayed for courage and God's protection before heading out. Alone.

My legs felt strong enough to control the pedals of the five-speed manual transmission. I drove cautiously out of the community. All was well. I neared the bridge just minutes away from the house. Breathing deeply and slowly, in and out, I gripped the steering wheel tightly with both hands and drove onto the bridge. It had a slight incline that marked the halfway point. As I drove down the other side, my focus was on the road ahead and the cars in the opposite lane. Then a calm, small voice said, *Look up into the mirror.* I looked into the rearview mirror. Behind me, I could see the height of the bridge and the beautiful blue skies that hung above it. Then I heard these comforting words: *It's all behind you now.* As I focused my gaze ahead once more, tears fell from my eyes.

I had finally crossed over and conquered my fear!

9. But Now My Eyes Have Seen You

Then Job replied to the LORD: "I know that you can do all things; no plan of yours can be thwarted... My ears had heard of you but now my eyes have seen you. Therefore I despise myself and repent in dust and ashes."(Job 42:1-2, 5-6 NIV)

A New Life

A couple of months had passed, and I moved back to my apartment. But things felt different there. It no longer felt like home. In the past, it had been a haven, a place of rest and safety for others and me. Now, it was no longer warm and welcoming. The entry felt cold and uninhabited. I wasn't quite sure why but this was not home as I knew it.

I continued to spend most days at Mama's house and on occasion would return to the apartment in the evenings. Sometimes the alone time in the apartment made me become anxious. I'd think about the comments people were making about my life regarding a "great call" (e.g., "God is going to use you," "God has a mighty plan for your life," "The Devil is mad at you," etc.). I didn't know what to do with these remarks. Some people suggested the accident had been a direct result of sin in my life. Others, however, believed that God loved me and that the attack had come from the enemy. I didn't understand what it all meant, but I soon became aware that all the storms in my life had been more than "bad luck." They had been warfare—spiritual warfare. Good versus evil.

Monica M. Johnson

Though walking in God's promise was still new to me, I felt in my heart that the accident had not been a punishment from God. Perhaps my redemption was a sign of His confidence in me. I was unsure but wanted to remain close to Him. I decided I would pray for peace and for answers. I often prayed that God would restore my memory and show me what it meant to be "used" by Him.

The people of the church in Brandywine, MD, had become the folks I called my family. The teachings there had set a strong foundation for my new walk as a believer. But, like my apartment, it no longer felt like home. The family there had embraced me and supported me through the years with their prayers. They had given my family great support during and after the accident. Though they were dear to my heart, my time there seemed to be ending. I needed more so that I could understand what was happening in my life and where this calling was taking me.

All Along

One day, after praying to God about the "great call," I called a devout woman of God I had come to know through the church. Her lifestyle reflected a level of true intimacy with God. She was slow to speak and quick to listen. She told me the story of Mary, Jesus' mother. She emphasized the fact that Mary had found favor in God's eyes. She said to me, "Just as God found one to carry His Word in the Bible days, God found you to carry His Word now, in the present time." She said that I was "the apple of His eye." An interesting choice of words.

> *My steps have held to your paths; my feet have not slipped.*
> *I call on you, O God, for you will answer me; give ear to me and hear my prayer.*
> *Show the wonder of your great love, you who save by your right hand those who take refuge in you from their foes.*
> *Keep me as the apple of your eye; hide me in the shadow of your wings from the wicked who assail me, from my mortal enemies who surround. (Psalms 17:1–9, NIV)*

For years I'd been praying to be the apple of my daddy's eye, and now I was being told that I was the apple of God's eye.

> *Just as we protect the pupils ("apples") of our eyes, so God will protect us. (Psalm 17:8, Life Application Bible NIV Tyndale Commentary Copyright 1989)*

God had protected me in the midst of the storms of my life. God really did care for me. He was present and there was no need to feel ashamed for confessing my faith in a God who hadn't stopped the accident from happening and allowed me to sense His presence along the journey.

I was ready to serve.

More than Enough

My emptiness and longing for something more had become my past. Jesus was now more than the God I had heard about—He was the God I had experienced while in the storm. Each victory within the storm had strengthened me mentally, spiritually, and physically.

But I was still being tested.

Monica M. Johnson

The next storm came in the form of dealing, once again, with fear. Despite all the positive reports from the doctors, I felt increasingly fearful of the unknown. I started believing that I hadn't been fully healed. I had distressing thoughts of being in another car accident and not pulling through it this time. Although I tried with all my might to believe that the thoughts that plagued my mind weren't true, I couldn't defeat them. They taunted me daily.

Without realizing it, I was doubting what I had come to know as God's power, and His ability to sustain my healing. I started thinking that I was destined to live a life of sorrow and suffering in order to be "used." This "call" had become a great burden, and I wanted to run far away from whatever it meant. The mental distress adversely affected my body. Suddenly, there was pressure in my chest and it was difficult to breathe. I couldn't help thinking that my lungs were about to collapse again. I was ashamed to be doubting and questioning just days after receiving signs and miracles of his presence. After all, I had proclaimed that God had healed me. I had accepted that I was the "apple of His eye." Why was I so quick to fear?

So I sat alone in my apartment. I was ashamed to share my fears and doubts with anyone. Though it was painful to internalize them, I remained isolated and attempted to pray more. To hope more. Night after night, alone in my apartment, I was determined not to be defeated and set back. I had to know that God was more than enough to keep my mind clear and to keep me safe.

Desperately, I continued to war with myself.

Out of Nowhere

On this particular morning, I experienced what felt like a fresh start. I'd been sitting in my bedroom relaxing. The doubts and fears hadn't been governing my mind. Then I left to go to Mama's house. As I pulled into her driveway, the school bus arrived, and Walter and my nephew Jarren got off. I decided I would take them to get a snack at McDonald's. They excitedly jumped into my car, and off we went.

After picking up some food, we went to a nearby park, Jonas Green, to eat. It was near the Naval Academy, and beneath the bridge on which I'd had the car accident. It was warm out. A perfect day to sit outside. Once the kids had eaten their food and finished their homework, they played along the shore. I watched them attentively as they carved figures in the wet sand, waded in the water, and collected stones, sticks, and shells. There was no one else around. I embraced the moment of stillness and took in the scene: the sailboats, the birds, the waves, the trees, and the beautiful houses along the shoreline.

Suddenly, out of nowhere, a man appeared. He was in his late sixties or early seventies and wearing faded blue-jean overalls and a white T-shirt. Wanting to be alone, I turned my head away, hoping that he would avoid approaching me. But he didn't. He greeted me and asked how I was doing. I didn't want to be rude, so I gave him a short response. He wasn't bothered by my lack of interest in him. He asked if I was a Christian. I hesitated and then turned toward him. I looked him in the eyes in an attempt to find out what he really wanted from me.

"Yes," I finally replied.

He nodded. "I could tell because of the aura around you." I was momentarily stunned. Then he asked, "Are you a teacher?"

Looking back to the water to check on the kids, I said no. Shy and reserved, I couldn't imagine myself in front of any kind of audience. Again he stunned me with his response.

"You'll become one someday."

He continued. He said that the Lord knew of my yearnings, my disappointments, and my concerns about my calling. Then he reassured me that God was with me. He said that I would soon leave my church (in Brandywine) and that that would be okay. He also spoke of my attire, saying that I wouldn't be able to dress the way that I was dressed (referring to my short cut-off shorts)

Monica M. Johnson

as a woman of God. He talked about my future in ministry and marriage. He explained that the man who was currently interested in me was not the man God had for me. The man might be what I wanted, but he wasn't what I needed. The stranger said that God would give me what I wanted and needed in a relationship.

I tried to argue with him, but he wouldn't engage. He kindly continued, seemingly on some kind of an assignment to get this message to me. Next, he shared that I would have a worldwide healing ministry, and that this ministry would be different than most.

As he spoke, I continued to keep a watchful eye on the kids, who were now feeding the ducks along the shore. Suddenly, the stranger grabbed my full attention by saying in a calm, reassuring, yet authoritative voice, "Don't worry about them. I have them."

Normally, it would have gone against my better judgment to trust a stranger—especially one who was telling me he was watching my kids while staring me in the face. But instead of questioning his ability to do such a thing, I gave him my full attention. I was tuned in to the words of this stranger.

He said that God loved me, and that I had considered turning my back on God. Immediately, I thought that he had to be crazy. I confidently told him that he wasn't correct. I thought about how much God had done in my life, and how I would never turn my back on Him. After I finished my thought, he said slowly, and almost in a whisper, "You thought about turning your back on the Lord." He nodded once, as if to say, *Think about it, Monica.*

His gentle nod gave me an understanding of what he was talking about. The week prior, I'd been giving in to the fears and doubts and wanting to run from "being used" by God. The stranger was correct. I had thought about turning back.

He continued to speak. His knowledge about my life was stunning. He spoke about my car accident—information I hadn't shared with him. He said that my healing had been divine and that if I turned my back on the Lord I would die. "I'm not trying to scare you," he explained. "But your body belongs to the Lord, and God wants to use you and your testimony."

I didn't know if the stranger was referring to a physical death or a spiritual death/separation from God. I was well aware that a spiritual death was far worse than a physical death. Spending even one day without God was a frightening thought to me. I began to weep. I wanted to control my emotions but couldn't.

Finally, the stranger told me that he had endured two car accidents, and that God had healed him. He told me of all the injuries he'd sustained. While he was on the operating table, a light came through the room (healing him instantly) and the doctors had to close him up immediately. The doctors had shared the amazing story with him, and told him they were shocked by his miraculous healing. (My initial thought was *Oh, Lord, I sure hope you're not telling me that I'll have to endure a second car accident.* To my relief, that wasn't the point the stranger was making!) He said, "You've been crying all week because the enemy told you that you aren't healed." For a moment, in shock, I was unable to breathe. "I want you to know that *when God heals you, YOU ARE HEALED!*"

Then the tears poured down my face. I dropped my head and covered my face with my hands. The stranger stood at arm's length in front of me, still and quiet. As I lifted my head and wiped my face, he asked if he could pray for me. Somehow, through the lump in my throat, I uttered yes. He gently placed his hand on my head and prayed. His prayer was like a balm that soothed my entire being. His words brought me comfort and healing.

Monica M. Johnson

As he began to walk away, I became aware of my surroundings again. The kids were in plain view and safe. I glanced away from them to say thank you to the stranger, but he was gone. He had disappeared as quickly as he had appeared. When I asked the kids what they'd thought about the stranger, they said they hadn't seen him.

I dropped the kids off at Mama's because I needed time to process what had happened. Back at my apartment, I wrote about the experience in my journal. It was incredible to know that the Lord loved me so much that He would send a stranger to ease my mind during my time of distress. Then a dark voice spoke: "He wasn't of God." A little shaken, I immediately asked the Lord to please show me if it was okay to believe what the stranger had said to me. I grabbed my Bible and opened it. Not having a great knowledge of the scriptures, I was about to flip to the concordance in the back when my eyes were drawn to the open page. It said:

> *You may say to yourselves, "How can we know when a message has not been spoken by the Lord?" If what a prophet proclaims in the name of the Lord does not take place or come true, that is a message the Lord has not spoken. That prophet has spoken presumptuously. Do not be afraid of him.*
> *(Deuteronomy 18:21–22, NIV)*

My questioning stopped, and my fear went away. I realized that time would tell if the stranger's words had come from the Lord.

Shortly after the experience at the water, I left the church I'd called home for the past few years. It wasn't an easy step to take because there were those who made comments that made me feel guilty for leaving. But I was hungry for truths and thirsty for purposeful living. Moving forward gave me an inner peace that allowed me to learn and grow through other teachings. Although I didn't find a new church home immediately, each church I visited played an important part in revealing something about my call. Each church served as a place of rest, restoration, and nurturing.

I stopped running from being used by God. I didn't want to shun my calling out of fear. I realized I had been set apart for a divine purpose and didn't need to be afraid. I no longer felt a need to fit in with the crowd. I had let go of the many childhood beliefs that weren't founded in God's Word (the Bible). My mind seemed clearer. Now, I was hearing with my heart.

He Speaks

Although I was spending less time at church, my life was rich with spiritual insight. I learned to meditate on the things of God. One day, I decided to go to the water to relax—the same place where the stranger had visited me. As I walked the shoreline, tears in my eyes, I felt tremendous admiration for God's grace and compassion toward me. I was filled with gratitude that He was very near to me. He was felt in my renewed heart. Still, there was a slight sadness in me as I tried to understand why my childhood had been so tough and why God hadn't been with my family during those years. After all, Mama had prayed all the time. She had spent most of her time in the church. I was always angry and afraid during those years because of Daddy's drinking. As I questioned my childhood, my cry sounded like this:

Monica M. Johnson

Heavenly Father, I love you. I know that You love me. I know now that you hear me. And, Lord, I am grateful for having new life. I appreciate all that you've done. I know it was you who healed me and raised me up. But, Lord God, please help me understand what's going on in my life right now. There is still something missing. There is something I feel is available right before me, but I can't seem to reach it or come into its knowledge. I know I'm loved by you, and that that love is more than any love I've known. I know that I have found favor in your eyes, and I know that I am truly the apple of Your eye. If I can just figure out what is missing, I will be all right. If you would give me understanding, Lord.

I paused.

I know that you are real, that you are alive. I have seen all the miracles you performed. Yet...

I was afraid to ask the question, didn't want to sound ungrateful, but I couldn't rest. I had to ask.

Lord, why did you leave me and my family when I was younger? Why didn't you protect us from my father when he was drunk? Why didn't you keep us during those times? Why did you make us go through so much hell? Why didn't you listen to my prayers back then?

My eyes were full but for some reason I refused to cry. I didn't understand why He hadn't been present early in my life. I needed to know that God would remain faithful to me. Then one tear fell. I took a deep breath in. Unable to pace the shoreline any longer, I sat on the sand a few feet from the water. In my childhood, I'd had an image of God being unapproachable. I couldn't understand how a God who was so great and merciful to me now could have abandoned me in my youth. I was baffled.

As the wind blew softly across the water, everything became still. It was as if God Himself had been waiting for me to become quiet so that He could speak to me. As my heartbeat slowed and my mind grew silent, I heard the voice so clearly, so softly, and so sincerely. "I never left you."

> *So I will be with you; I will never leave you nor forsake you.*
> *(Joshua 1:5b, NIV)*

A second tear trickled down my face. The soft voice canceled every doubt I had about whether God would remain with me in my future. If He hadn't spoken another word concerning my questions about the past, His presence would have been enough for me to move forward. I was aware of His presence, and it yielded great comfort. I didn't understand how the power of His words had changed things in an instant, but they had. I felt safe. Reassured, even. Yet, He continued to speak!

The deceptions of my past were made clear. Each event of doubt that I'd had about God being present in my past played now, like a scene in a movie. I watched these events but it didn't hurt to recall them. God had been there all along, but I hadn't been aware of His presence. He had been present in many forms.

He was in the tears that cleansed me. He was in my room, giving me the ability to lie down and rest on the nights I feared closing my eyes. He was in the people who came into my life and altered the direction of it. He was in every closed door, every opportunity not given. He was in every open door as well. He was in every hug that Mama gave. The list went on and on. Endlessly.

Monica M. Johnson

Every situation in my life was an opportunity for me to seek God, not an opportunity to blame God for the evil that was present. Each situation that caused me harm in some way (emotionally, physically, or spiritually) gave me the opportunity to grow and experience Him. I prayed to God and he always answered me: sometimes immediately, sometimes days, months, or even years later. At times, I missed His answers and truths because they weren't what I wanted to hear. Not all of the bad situations were a result of the Devil—I created some of them because of choices I made. Yet, God always answered me by giving me wisdom, direction, or simply a sense of peace so I could move forward. Each victory was an opportunity to become a witness to what God can do. (For more on this idea, I highly recommend reading Dave Earley's book *21 Reasons Bad Things Happen to Good People*.)

God never actually left me at all. He was always present.

> *If we are faithless, he will remain faithful, for he cannot disown himself.*
> *(2 Timothy 2:13, NIV)*

As tears gently rolled from my eyes, I looked up toward the sky. I realized that before, I'd had no idea how to identify God's presence in my life. I realized that my car accident hadn't been a sign of God's judgment but proof of God's confidence in me. Although I'd been raised in the church, I hadn't known Christ personally until I experienced Him through my tough times.

> *Remember, I am with you always, to the end of the age.*
> *(Matthew 28:20, NRSV)*

And so it was. God was with me. When Mama had told me to thank God in all situations, she'd meant I should invite Him into every situation. In the bad times, we must thank Him for His presence and guidance in advance. It is through His Holy Spirit that we are empowered and able to come through those difficult challenges in life.

God didn't change me when I wanted to be better because I hadn't truly invited Him into my life and learned His Word. The change would come through moving away from my old way of thinking and renewing my relationship with Him. My born-again experience required work on my part, not just a miraculous move on God's part. When I started really believing, and trusting the Holy Spirit, I made choices according to God's will for my life. I no longer made my own decisions, which often left me questioning what I was to do. There is a level of surrender required to see God's will unfold in your life. I hadn't fully surrendered upon giving my life to God and attending the classes required to "join the church."

In that moment by the water, my mind was incredibly at ease. The more I relaxed and trusted in the moment, the more He spoke and the clearer I could hear Him. My breathing changed as He continued to reveal Himself to me.

When situations turn dark, the Holy Spirit will strengthen us. God hadn't stopped my accident from occurring, so I'd had to trust Him through my healing process, no matter the end result.

When we pray that God's will be done, we may not get what we ask for, but if we are quiet long enough He will guide us through it.

Just as Job declared in the bible, now I can boldly say, "**My ears had heard of you, but now my eyes have seen You!**" I eagerly wait to see what the Lord will do. He is growing in my heart as never before.

Monica M. Johnson

As I sat on the shore beneath that bridge, the sun's rays heated the surface of the water and the grains of sand. The water and the ground embraced the sun's warmth and yielded an atmosphere of peace and tranquility. The blue skies, extending as far as the eye could see, welcomed the passing clouds. The wind blew ever so gently across my shoulders and my back.

I lifted my eyes to the sky. *The storm is over.*

> *Who is this? He commands even the winds and the water, and they obey him. (Luke 8:25b, NIV)*

EPILOGUE: The Storm Is Over

Many are the afflictions of the righteous, but the LORD delivers him out of them all.   *(Psalms 34:19, ESV)*

I Have Been Redeemed

My life is far richer because I know that my Savior Jesus Christ lives. I know that He loves me. He paid the price by dying on the cross for me so that I might live my life of purpose. When I overcame my afflictions, I surrendered my life to God, to show Him how much I loved Him. Now, I am perfect. I am perfectly complete in Him. "Be ye therefore perfect, even as your Father which is in heaven is perfect" (Matthew 5:48, KJV). He is perfecting His love in me. It is the latter part of my life that is more blessed because I have endured the storms and God has revealed to me who He is. In his book *In the Eye of the Storm*, pastor and author Max Lucado eloquently writes: "I saw God... The God who uses my storms as his path to come to me. I saw God. It took a storm for me to see him. But I saw him. And I'll never be the same."[1]

The experiences that fill this book now serve as markers on my journey. When I'm in trouble, stagnant, or challenged, or when my faith is tested, I'm able to return to this book and remember what God has done for me. And then I am strengthened. I can stand firm in my faith. Life isn't perfect for me now. I still have fears, and I don't claim to "have it all together." Challenges and

---

[1] Max Lucado, *In the Eye of the Storm* (Thomas Nelson, 2012), p. xx

Monica M. Johnson

negative situations still arise. I still feel sad and disappointed sometimes. I question things. But I have a relationship with the true and living God. I have Him to believe in, to experience, and to strengthen me in those challenging times. I live a life with purpose. I have been redeemed!

"**Redeem**" (from Merriam-Webster):

1. a: to buy back: repurchase [*Jesus Christ died on the cross*]

   b: to get or win back [*Jesus Christ won my lost soul*]

2. to free from what distresses or harms [*Jesus Christ delivered me from my life of sin, pleasures of the flesh, and destruction*]

I will go out into a world that is desperately in search of purpose, love, and peace, and I will offer it my greatest fulfillment: my Helper, my Comforter, God, Jesus, the Holy Spirit. I may not be able to teach everyone who begat whom within the scriptures, but I can share the beauty of God's love where I'm able.

We can go beyond simply existing. We can find purpose in our lives and ultimately enter into a relationship with a true and loving God.

I can hear the Father asking, "Who best to tell My story?" His answer, "You and I. We who have been redeemed by the hand of the Father."

Go tell His story, a story of Love to all the world.

A Final Note

This puzzle was moved from one hospital to another and then home, and it remained intact. How symbolic. Just as the pieces were collected and made into a perfect piece of art, my family remained a solid unit as they were challenged with difficult decisions concerning my well-being.

And like a puzzle, I have been put back together.

My body has recovered in ways the doctors said were impossible. My lungs are fully functioning. My bladder has completely healed. Although the doctors have said I will never have relations or additional children, my pelvis has realigned perfectly and no longer requires pins or plates. I don't walk with a limp or any kind of impairment. There are no secondary infections or complications. The sensation in my left hand has been completely restored. I delight in learning more sign language and look forward to eventually being used in the deaf community to share God's love.

Monica M. Johnson

My memory is improving daily. There is wholeness in my relationships with my son and immediate family. Most importantly, God's story remains perfect and is being perfected in us. We will go on to tell the story of God's undying love for us.

For I know that my Redeemer lives, and in the end he will stand upon the earth. (Job 19:25, NIV)

When caught in the storms of life, it is easy to think that God has lost control and that we're at the mercy of the winds of fate. In reality, God is sovereign. He controls the history of the world as well as our personal destinies. Just as Jesus calmed the waves, He can calm whatever storms you may face. (Luke 8:25cf, NIV)

Made in the USA
Middletown, DE
28 September 2019